UK AND IRELAND

CIRCUMNAVIGATOR'S GUIDE

SAM STEELE

ADLARD COLES • LONDON

**In memory of my Father who introduced me to the
Arthur Ransome books and taught me how to sail.**

Published by Adlard Coles Nautical
an imprint of A & C Black (Publishers) Ltd
36 Soho Square, London W1D 3QY
www.adlardcoles.com

First published 2008

ISBN: 978-0-7136-8886-3

A CIP catalogue record for this book is available from the British Library.

This book is produced using paper that is made from wood grown in
managed, sustainable forests. It is natural, renewable and recyclable.
The logging and manufacturing processes conform to the environmental
regulations of the country of origin.

Typeset in 10.5/12.5pt URWGroteskTLig by Margaret Brain

Printed and bound in Spain by GraphyCems

CONTENTS

INTRODUCTION

There are an increasing number of motorboats and yachts circumnavigating Britain and Ireland. To many sailors it is the trip of a lifetime, a real dream, but it can seem daunting. The year before our planned voyage, the weather forecasts seemed to show endless gales sweeping across Scotland. How would we cope in such conditions?

This was to be our first extended cruise but when we looked for advice we found little available on cruising in home waters. Most books are aimed at sailors preparing for blue water cruising and I avidly read many of them. But there was much relevant information for us missing, which was the reason why I was inspired to write this book. It is designed to fill in some of the gaps and I hope it whets your appetite to explore our wonderful coastline.

Whether you own a motorboat or yacht, the planning and preparation are much the same and the aim of this guide is to help you to prepare successfully so that you can make the most of your circumnavigation. It is surprising how much work has to be done in advance for a trip like this. There is new equipment to fit, stores to buy and stow, charts and pilot books to source, to name just a few of the tasks. I describe our methods but also explain what we would have done differently.

Since returning from the voyage, I have researched a number of other circumnavigations and obtained information from about 64 boatowners: 50 in yachts, 11 in motorboats and 3 in RIBs. The experiences and advice of these sailors, added to my own knowledge, has enabled me to compile this guide for all would-be circumnavigators.

The term 'Round Britain' can be used to describe many routes, though strictly speaking, it includes all the islands out to Rockall and Muckle Flugga but excludes the Channel Islands and Northern Ireland. If you do not include the Islands on your route, it is only a circumnavigation around mainland Britain. Taking a route through the canals technically cannot be called 'Round Britain'; however, in this book I refer to a trip via the Caledonian Canal as 'Round Britain' as it is a recognised route.

Many websites have been included in the book to provide additional information and, at the time of publication, they were correct. However, the internet is constantly changing and a site which may appear today may have gone or changed tomorrow. If the address is no longer valid, use a search engine to locate the new one.

My mate Mags and I sailed our circumnavigation in our jointly owned Rival 38 *Ituna*, built in 1977. Mags holds the RYA Day Skipper qualification and has gained most of her experience on our short summer cruises around the French coast, the Channel Islands and the west coast of England. I started sailing on the Norfolk Broads in my home-built Mirror dinghy. I progressed to yachts and gained the RYA Yachtmaster Offshore qualification at the age of 20. I have since enjoyed cruising around the Baltic Sea, France, the Channel Islands, Canaries and the Azores.

When we bought our boat, the idea was to go off cruising for a year but we quickly discovered that saving money and owning a boat seemed to be incompatible. We managed to arrange four months leave from our jobs so sticking to home waters seemed the best plan. Another reason for our choice of trip is that Mags suffers from seasickness as soon as the sea state is declared to be 'slight'. So committing to a year, with long passages, would have really been her idea of torture. So we decided on a circumnavigation with coastal hops. This book should give hope to all those who are stuck with the dreaded malaise… you do eventually get your sea-legs!

I grew up with the stories of my heroes such as Sir Francis Chichester and have always wanted to go off on my own adventure but I am, by nature, cautious. This circumnavigation was our big challenge and at the back of my mind was the thought; 'Could we do it?' But on 1 May 2006 we set off from Gosport and sailed clockwise around Britain, arriving back safely on 23 August. So if we can do it – so can you!

Sam Steele

Ituna ghosting past the Spey Bay, Moray Firth.
Photo: Klaus Schroeter

ACKNOWLEDGEMENTS

I would like to thank all the circumnavigators that answered my questions; I enjoyed reliving the trip through their stories and logs. Thanks also go to the people that replied to my questions but did not want their names mentioned.

Yachts
Charlie Tait, David and Mary Trim *Jemina Onvi* 385
Gordon Stollard *Pipe Dream* Island Packet 420
Sam Kent *Silverwind* Hunter Delta 25
Sid and Margaret Hygate *Kiddet* Halmatic 30
Clive Anstiss and Les Sutcliffe *Quintet* Freeman 30
David Rainsbury *Piper* Contessa 26
Geoffrey Palmer *Shardik* Contessa 32
John Hill *Almacantar* Hustler 38
Carol and Dermot Stewart *Gemini* Beneteau 31
Denis Argent *Dorran* Rival 34
David Buckpitt *Nefertiti of St Helier* 62ft Ketch
Sarah Fagg *Huffin* Hurley 22
Steve and Claire Crook *Touché* Beneteau 36
Greg, Sue, Kate and Sebastian Hill *Blue Argolis* Trewes 41
Bill and Anita Miller *Marika M* Westerly Corsair
Stan Lester *Indalo* Mirage 2700
Chester Wallace *Bellini* Moody 336
Karen Hodges *Loon at Sea* Caprice 18
Mike Dixon *Gellie Fairey* Atalanta 31
Vince Spooner *Anita A* Contessa 26
Iain and Penny Kidson *Rainbow Catcher* Gemini 33
Tony Brimble *Gitana* Crealock 34
Geoff Holt *Freethinker* Challenger tri 15ft
Mike Fellows *Kes* Van de Stadt 28
Jonathan Hutchinson *Zia Maria* Moody 31
Irving Benjamin *Vega* LM Vitesse 33 who is still en route.
Steve Cooksey *Gamaldansk* Westerly GK29
Tom Cunliffe *Hirta* 50ft Gaff Cutter who has completed the trip twice.
Rob Jenkins *Deerhunter* Hunter Medina 20
Nico Shipman *Gothik* Westerly GK29

Motor Boats

Dominic and Gribbin *Jura Pilot* Hardy Family pilot 20
Mike, Michelle, Letitia and Michael Perry *Caribbean Breeze* Fairline 36 Turbo
Malcolm and Glenda Stennett *Lady Genevieve* Broom 39 and Broom 44 – they have completed the trip three times.

My thanks also go to Simon Keeling from Weather Consultancy for reading the weather sections. It was also thanks to him that we missed a huge storm, in which a Brittany Ferry was damaged at sea; we were able to leave our anchorage at Fishguard and make it up to Holyhead before the storm hit.

Also my thanks to Sandy Campbell, who helped set up our website and managed it for us during our trip, and for his help in writing the chapter Staying in Touch. And last, but by no means least, thanks go to Mags, who made this trip possible and for her patience when I was writing this book.

QUOTES FROM CIRCUMNAVIGATORS

What were our highlights?

'Scottish lochs – tranquillity and stunning scenery'
John Hill *Almacantar* Hustler 38

'Eastern Ireland and western Scotland – wonderful cruising, weather and very welcoming'
Chester Wallace *Bellini* Moody 336

'Superb night sail from Milford to Arklow; the friendly folk we met; the Caledonian and Crinan Canals'
Sid Hygate *Kiddet* Halmatic 30

'Everything! Great trip – wildlife: whales, dolphins and puffins'
Mike Perry *Caribbean Breeze* Fairline 36

'The friendliness of everyone we met'
Denis Argent *Dorran* Rival 34

'So many! Anchoring outside the Humber to wait for the tide and finding ourselves surrounded by about 30 seals who played for hours; the satisfaction of making it to the Orkneys; the Western Isles – beautiful sailing and scenery.'
Sarah Fagg *Huffin* Hurley 22

'Gannets on Grassholme and Bass Rock; otters in Scotland; dolphins; Tall Ships in Waterford; the isolation of the Western Isles; hospitality in Ireland; sense of achievement with partner.'
Steve and Claire Crook *Touché* Beneteau 36

1

IS THIS THE VOYAGE FOR ME?

How many times have you finished your annual cruise and thought, 'if only I could continue sailing a bit longer?' Or maybe it was after reading an article in a boating magazine that you dreamt of a real adventure in your boat. However, for many the dream never becomes reality because time is limited. But to sell up and head off into the blue yonder is a brave step to take. But if you want to try a taster to see if living on your boat appeals to you then perhaps a cruise around the UK could be the answer as it offers several advantages:

- You never have to decide at what point you have to turn back, as you just keep going round the coast.
- With many harbours and anchorages to choose from, you have the ability to coastal hop, with only a few long passages required.
- You are never too far from home, in case of an emergency.
- You don't have to sell your house to complete the voyage.
- You don't need to be as self sufficient for maintenance, as you would on a longer blue water cruise, as most harbours have some skilled mechanics.
- There are no language issues, which does make it much easier to understand the weather forecasts.
- As the cruise is for a short period, you may be able to get a sabbatical from your job. Having a guaranteed job to come back to considerably reduces the financial risks.

NOT JUST A HOLIDAY!

Your circumnavigation is not just a holiday, you will experience:

+ Hard work, with lots of early starts to catch the tide.
+ Tight schedules. Depending on your time available, you will always be thinking about pressing on, so that you are back home at the right time.
+ Challenging tides and navigation.

But the rewards are:

Sunrise over Dover

+ Awesome scenery – our coastline is truly beautiful.
+ Spectacular sunrises – just rewards for those early starts.
+ An abundance of wildlife which can be seen at close quarters.
+ Many new friendships will be made along the way.
+ An incredible sense of achievement.

We now watch the TV weather forecasts and see the map of the UK with a sense of pride – it is great to see exactly where we sailed, recognising each bump on our coastline.

IS OWNING A BOAT ESSENTIAL?

If you don't own a boat, you can still circumnavigate. There are several sailing schools that offer a 'round Britain experience', either as part of a Yachtmaster ™ fast track course or a mile-builder. Their trips last from six weeks to three months. We met one couple who had chartered a boat with a skipper for eight weeks and successfully completed the trip via the Caledonian Canal. They showed an adventurous spirit, as neither of them had much offshore experience prior to their trip. Though they did feel that after the trip, they would know what qualities they were looking for in a boat.

RACING OR CRUISING?

I have assumed that most readers will be cruising but if you are interested in racing then there are several races open for motorboats and yachts. However, not all are open to amateur entrants. If you really feel the need for speed then there are many records that have been set. Though you will have to be flying to beat the current records: in a power boat it is 27 hours 10 minutes for a round-Britain voyage. If sailing, you will need to be clocking up an average speed of nearly 16 knots to complete a 'round Britain and Ireland' in 4 days 16 hours.

WHAT SIZE BOAT DO YOU NEED?
Many sizes of boat have been used to complete the trip (see Acknowledgements).

Yachts
The smallest yacht was 18ft (5.5m) right up to 62ft (19m). The largest boat to be sailed single-handedly for the whole trip was 28ft (8.5m), though most boats less than 26ft (8m) were sailed solo. The average size of the yachts was 32ft (9.7m). The smallest yacht to be sailed via Cape Wrath was a 20ft (6m), Hunter Medina 20, *Deerhunter*.

Motor boats
The boats ranged from 20 to 48ft (6 to 14.6m) and the average size was 36ft (11m). The smallest motor boat which made it successfully around via Cape Wrath was a 20ft (6m).

RIBs
The ribs varied in size between 28 and 31ft (8.5 and 9.5m).

Other craft
Most would consider a circumnavigation in a reasonable-sized boat a challenge. For some that is not enough; smaller boats completing the trip included:

Dinghy Ron Pattenden, sailed round Britain in a 13ft (4m) Laser dinghy in 2004; his diary was featured in *Yachts and Yachting*.

Duart Castle, Mull

Kayak There have been a few voyages by kayak and many of their stories have been captured in books or on websites; their details are in Appendix 4.

Windsurfer Tim Batstone, circumnavigated Britain in 1984 on a 12ft (3.7m) windsurfer.

Sunset over Mull, from Puilladobhrain

GOALS

Whilst researching this book, I have come across many different goals which inspired such an adventure:

- To be the fastest circumnavigator.
- To race others.
- To see the scenery and wildlife.
- To experience new places.
- To gain sailing experience and test your seamanship skills.
- To gain a qualification.
- To challenge yourself physically.
- To raise money for charity.
- To find freedom outside your physical boundaries
- And just because the cruise appeals to you.

There are probably many others but, whatever your goal, you need to have a common understanding with your crew if you are going to make the voyage a success. Your goals will help your decision-making process along the way, eg, whether to sail, how long to spend in a location etc. Dissimilar goals will lead to friction, as your crew will have different expectations and may not understand or agree with the decisions you make. When Vivien Cherry skippered the Global Challenge boat *Cooper's & Lybrand* around the world, friction arose due to the skipper's goal being to 'race around the

COURAGE AND DETERMINATION

For most people this trip will be a real adventure, the challenge of a lifetime. However, one group of people have so much courage and determination that they have found freedom, through canoeing or sailing, to overcome their disabilities.

✦ *Nigel Rogoff*, who lost his leg in a parachuting display, completed a trip around Britain in 2002 in a kayak. His companion *David Abrutat*, paralysed in a car crash, accompanied him on a handcycle on the coastal roads.

✦ *Geoff Holt* was paralysed from the chest down and confined to a wheelchair, after a swimming accident. He successfully completed his trip round Britain via the Caledonian Canal, in his trimaran dinghy *Freethinker* in 109 days visiting 51 places and 51 days at sea. Not only did he sail round Britain in the summer of 2007, which was a challenging year for weather, it was also an impressive logistical exercise. He had a support team of seven, three vehicles and a RIB. Geoff aptly describes this as his personal Everest; his journey can be found at www.personaleverest.com.

✦ *Hillary Lister* is quadriplegic and is only able to move her head. In 2005, she sailed into the record books when she went solo across the English Channel by using a 'sip and puff' system of straws to control the sails and tiller. Just prior to publication Hilary attempted a solo circumnavigation round Britain in an Artemis 20, a 20ft (6.1m) carbon fibre performance keelboat. See her story at www.hilarylister.com.

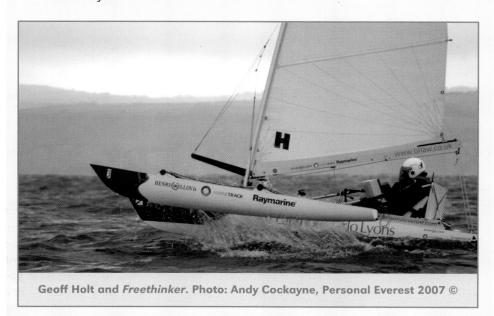

Geoff Holt and *Freethinker*. Photo: Andy Cockayne, Personal Everest 2007 ©

world', and some of the crew, whose aim was to 'sail around the world'. These are conflicting goals; one requires that you constantly drive the boat to maximize your speed, and the other is about enjoying life onboard at a more relaxed pace.

For us, part of the joy of extended cruising was to get away from the stresses of our daily lives. Work is driven by targets, so we wanted to be careful to avoid setting tough targets for our time off. We could have been unlucky and had to turn back due to lack of time because of bad weather. Once people know what your goals are, if you fail to complete them, some may think you have failed, even if you had a great cruise. When people asked us where we were going, we used to say that we are going out of the harbour and turning right. Well for 51 days, we turned right and on 3 days, we turned left!

WHAT EXPERIENCE DO YOU NEED?

Good seamanship is essential for this trip. Our coast, whilst spectacular, is full of dangers: You will experience strong tides (the Orkneys see spring tides of 12 knots); the treacherous sandbanks (those of the North Sea can uncover 20 miles out to sea) plus navigation between rocks, and that is before you add the weather and other vessels. Clearly, a RYA Yachtmaster™ or similar qualification and experience will help. However, competing this cruise successfully is much more than having a certain qualification or a defined number of years experience. Some of the additional skills you will need are:

➤ *Maintenance* Using your boat for an extended period means that you need to keep both it and its equipment working. It is important that you are able to carry out basic fault-finding and servicing on your engine.

➤ *Living on board* This small hole in the water surrounded by fibreglass, plastic or wood will be your home for the extended period. Conditions can range from primitive camping to a very comfortable caravan, depending on your budget. Whichever you chose, you have to be able to live in the confined space that you have.

➤ *Cooking* Food is your fuel and hot food is especially important on those cold wet days. You must be disciplined in order to feed and hydrate your body. After a long tiring passage, it is easy to miss meals because you are too tired to cook. Dehydration can be debilitating, and is a very real danger even in cold climes. Even being slightly dehydrated every day can build up into a problem.

➤ *Crew bonding* A boat is a very small place if you fall out with your fellow sailors; you must choose your crew carefully. If you are going on a trip which is organised by others, you should feel confident that you will get on with the rest of the crew.

➤ *Management* The whole trip will require good planning and preparation. You can have all the sailing experience in the world but a poorly planned cruise, and an ill-prepared boat, is unlikely to result in a successful trip. Hopefully, the next few chapters will help you to get well organised.

2

PLANNING THE ROUTE

HOW MUCH TIME DO YOU NEED?

For most people the length of the cruise is likely to be dictated by factors such as work, finance etc. Therefore, it will have to be a balance between the route and the number of stops. There are several options:

➤ England and lowland Scotland via the Forth and Clyde Canal
➤ England, Ireland and Lowland Scotland via the Forth and Clyde Canal
➤ Britain via Cape Wrath
➤ Britain via the Caledonian Canal
➤ UK and Ireland via Cape Wrath

Obviously, the more time you have, the more places you can visit and the shorter the legs; there is also the greater chance that you can pick and chose your weather windows. You may also decide to press on quickly through areas that you know well, or take on additional crew to do some long initial legs to allow you to spend more time cruising new areas. The shorter your time frame, the greater will be the pressure to keep moving. Even with a four-month cruise you will still feel the pressure to keep moving on whenever you can.

If you take the inside route through the Irish Sea up to the Minch, then Ireland and the Outer Hebrides will protect you from the Atlantic swell. Circumnavigating Ireland adds an additional 300 miles to your trip but you also need to take into account the weather and Atlantic swell. You will see from graphs 1 and 2 (page 12) that Malin Head has the highest number days of summer gales of all the reference points chosen round the UK and Ireland.

If time is running short, the Caledonian Canal offers a way of saving time. It is 50 nautical miles long and will save you approximately 250 to 500 miles depending on the number of stops you make. It can be done in 2–3 days, though your licence allows you 8 days in the canal. The benefit comes not only from the shorter distance; it is also more sheltered, though the wind can be funnelled down the glens. So the wind will either be with you or against you and in fresh water the wind can cause quite a chop. There are other options if time is short: England and lowland Scotland via the Forth and Clyde Canal, or round Ireland, or round Scotland, though strictly speaking it is only part of Scotland. This route is approximately 690nm.

We completed the round Britain trip in 4 months – a total of 114 days. We were at sea for 54 days with an average passage length of 41 miles and visited 53 places. We decided to take a 10-day holiday in the Orkneys, after all, cruising can be hard work! The remaining 50 days in harbour were due to either bad weather, needing to catch up with boat tasks or just sight-seeing. Yet an identical boat to ours completed a similar route in 20 days, with only 4 stops on the Round Britain Race. We left north-west Scotland with a feeling that we had just had a taster and that there was still so much to be seen. It was difficult to decide what to miss out on the west coast of Scotland, given the huge choice of islands and anchorages. There were fewer suitable ports on the east coast but it does mean more opportunities for meeting people on similar trips.

Circumnavigation time survey

I found in my survey that the length of time spent at sea varied considerably. Greg and Sue Hill (*Blue Argolis* Trewes 41) completed the same route in the school holidays, in just over 6 weeks, of which 28 days were at sea, they visited 14 places en route. At the other end of the scale, Steve and Claire Crook (*Touché* Beneteau 36), took 2 summers and visited 133 places, but even they said they had not had time to see everything that they wanted to. When asked what they would do differently, they said 'take 3 summers'!

My survey of circumnavigating yachts showed the following:

Route by yacht and number of boats	Average				
	Logged (nm)	Passage length (nm)	Cruise duration (days)	Days at sea	Number of places visited
England and lowland Scotland via the Forth and Clyde Canal (1)	1561	27	92	58	47
England, Ireland and Lowland Scotland via the Forth and Clyde Canal (1)	1700	27	108	64	62
Britain via Cape Wrath (25)	2202	41	88	54	56

Route by yacht and number of boats	Average				
Britain via the Caledonian Canal (18)	1856	40	89	47	43
UK and Ireland via Cape Wrath (5)	2541	50	85	51	48
Ireland (4)	1100	37	33	30	26

For motorboats, the average number of days at sea is relatively high but this is over a small number of boats. The quickest motorboat was Mike Perry and his family (*Caribbean Breeze* Fairline 36); they completed their trip via the Caledonian Canal in 98 hours, after 21 days at sea and total cruise length of 38 days with 18 stops. However, when asked what he would do differently he said 'take longer and make more stops'. At the other end of the scale Dominic and Nicola Gribbin (*Jura Pilot* Hardy Family Pilot 20) cruised for 18 weeks, visiting 57 places and spending a total of 58 days at sea on their trip via Cape Wrath.

Route by motor boat	Average					
	Type and number of boats	Logged nm	Passage length (nm)	Cruise duration (days)	Days at sea	Number of places visited
Britain via Cape Wrath	Motor boat (6)	2113	59	64	36	42
	RIB (2)	1915	101	28	19	17
Britain via the Caledonian Canal	Motor boat (5)	1597	73	30	22	29
UK and Ireland via Cape Wrath	RIB (1)	2000	286	8	7	7

Can the trip be done in stages?

If you are not able to take much time off, it is possible to split the trip up and complete it in stages. This also gives you the ability to base your boat in a new location and enjoy exploring the area from that base, before moving on. The April and May 2006 editions of *Yachting Monthly* featured the story of a couple, John and Sue Chadwick (*Stromboli*, Saltram 36), who completed a trip via the Caledonian Canal. They broke up the route into 13 legs, taking 27 days and 4 nights, spread over a 13 month period. If you have a motorboat, it is very feasible to complete the cruise in stages. *Motor Boat and*

Yachting (February, March and April 1996) published accounts by Maurice and Wendy Walmsley (*Mors* Broom 37) and Malcolm and Glenda Stennett (*Lady Genevieve* Broom 39) about their trip round Britain via Cape Wrath. Splitting the journey up into 6 legs, they completed the trip in 31 days at sea, leaving the boat in Hull, Peterhead, Craobh Haven (pronounce 'Croove'), Inverkip, Dartmouth and finally returning to Southampton.

If you are planning a trip in stages, there are two things that you need to consider:

➤ Where you will leave the boat to make sure it is secure.
➤ Transport links to and from your boat.

If you are planning to leave the boat in a marina, you will find that in the north-west of Scotland, marinas and pontoons are limited. Between Oban and the Orkneys, marinas are only located at Kerrera (near Oban), Dunstaffnage, Stornoway and the Orkneys; though there are plans to open a marina in Ullapool in the future. There are similar challenges in the north-west of Ireland, where there are no marinas between Galway and Lough Swilly, though planning permission has been granted for a marina in Killybegs. You also need to plan transport to and from your boat. A summary of main marina locations, facilities and transport is in Appendix 3.

When should you leave?

The main factor that will influence your decision is the weather. April to the end of October seems to be the slot that most people pick and looking at graphs 1 and 2, you can see why. March has three times more gales than April, and November has nearly twice as many gales as October and two and a half times more than September. My survey showed that the most common time for yachts to leave was the first two weeks of May; over a third left then and returned in August. The motorboats that were on a longer cruise left in May but RIBs and those on a quick dash left in mid July.

WHICH WAY ROUND?

One of the biggest questions is: do you go left or right out of harbour? Two main factors will probably affect your decision.

Prevailing currents

The prevailing currents are relatively weak, with the rate of travel approximately 1.5nm per day (the apparent passage of an object). It favours a clockwise direction, with the exception of part of the south coast. On this stretch, you will carry the tide for longer, going anticlockwise. Likewise, from north-east England down to the Wash, there is a noticeably longer tide, favouring a southerly route.

Prevailing wind

There are two critical factors when looking at the prevailing wind: direction and percentage occurrence. A wind may blow from one direction more frequently than from

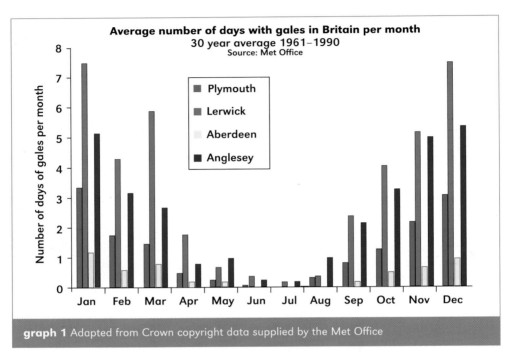

graph 1 Adapted from Crown copyright data supplied by the Met Office

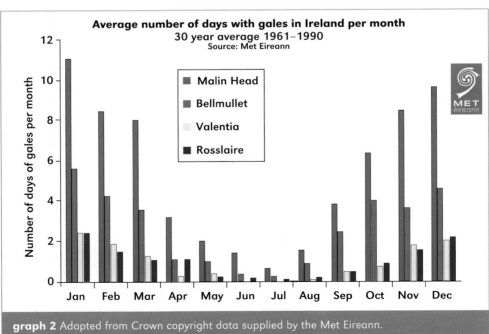

graph 2 Adapted from Crown copyright data supplied by the Met Eireann.

others; however, if its occurrence is low it means that it is not consistent from that direction. Some parts of the world never have wind from certain sectors. However, for a circum-navigation, the challenge is that the percentage occurrence from March to October, from any particular sector (45°) is relatively low. In May, when most people leave, the highest occurrence of any particular wind sector in the UK and Irish waters is on the Irish west coast, where there is a 21 per cent chance of a westerly wind. This also means that there is a 79 per cent chance that the wind is coming from a different direction! The occurrence increases if you look at a quarter, rather than a sector. The highest in May, is again off the west Irish coast, where the occurrence of a westerly or south-westerly is still only 36 per cent. This does also mean that you have the possibility of making progress against the prevailing wind, if you have enough time to wait.

However, here is a word of caution about theoretical calculations. These are averages over many years, but

General near-surface pattern of water movement around UK and Ireland from *Atlas of Seas around the British Isles*, © **Crown copyright (MAFF 1981)**

you will just be passing through the area and are very unlikely to spend a month seeing all the wind sectors. Unseasonal weather does happen; you have often heard weather forecasters say that a particular month is the wettest or hottest since records began. Local variation is another factor; the figures used are averages over a large sea area and coastal areas have more variation due to the effects of the land. Even if the wind is in the right direction, you then need to consider the swell. We were pinned down in Whitby for six days with strong north-easterly winds in August. Yet according to the figures, this was unlikely to happen. Once the storm abated, it was another two days before it was safe to leave the harbour because of the swell in the shallow entrance.

Table 1 shows the most common wind direction grouped by percentage of likely occurrence. In order to reduce the complexity of the table, I have not included any winds whose occurrence is 10 per cent or less but that doesn't mean that they don't occur.

	Percentage occurrence	April	May	June	July	Aug	Sep
England: east coast	21–25				SW	SW	SW
	16–20	NE	NE, SW	SW		W	
	11–15	E, SW		N, NE	W	NW	W, NW
England: south coast	21–25				SW, W	W	
	16–20		SW	W		SW	W
	11–15	NE, E, SW, W, NW	W, NW	NE, SW	NW		SW, NW
Irish Sea	21–25					SW	SW
	16–20					W	W
	11–15	N, NE, SW, NW	N, NE, S, SW, W, NW	SW, W, NW	N, S, SW, W, NW	NW, S	S, NW
Ireland: south coast	21–25					SW, W	
	16–20		SW, W	SW, W	SW, W		SW, W
	11–15	N, NE, S, SW, W	NE, NW	NW	S, NW	S, NW	S, NW
Ireland: west coast	21–25		W		W	W	
	16–20	N		SW, W	SW	SW	W, SW
	11–15	NE, S, SW, W	N, S, SW, NW	NW	S, NW	S, NW	S, NW
Outer Hebrides	21–25						
	16–20					SW, W	SW
	11–15	E, SW, W, NW	NE, SE, S, SW	SW, W, NW	N, S, SW, W, NW	S, NW	S, W, NW
Orkney Islands	21–25						
	16–20				W		S, SW
	11–15	N, SE, S, SW, W, NW	S, SE	N, S	N, SE, S, SW, NW	SE, S, SW, W, NW	SE, W

TABLE 1 Wind direction and percentage occurrence extracted from the Admiralty *Atlantic Routing Charts*. Adapted from © Crown Copyright data supplied by the Met Office.

Whitby, the day after the storm in August

Starting point
Scotland's best months for weather are May, June and early July. Ireland's driest time of the year is spring and the sunniest month is May. If you want to take advantage of these conditions, your starting point may influence which direction you go in.

CLOCKWISE v ANTICLOCKWISE
These general advantages apply to any Round Britain route, regardless of starting point.

General advantages of clockwise
The prevailing current favours a clockwise direction.

General advantages of anticlockwise
➤ Tacking across the Irish Sea allows good progress against the prevailing S, SW and W winds.
➤ You will enjoy the east coast first and then be even more impressed by the west coast.
➤ If a sea breeze forms on the east coast, it is likely to veer parallel to the coast with you during the day.

STARTING POINTS			
	Start point: south	**Start point: east**	**Start point: west**
Prevailing wind	No real advantage to clockwise or anti-clockwise route. There is a 2% advantage* favouring an anticlockwise direction but this is so low as to be considered statistically irrelevant.	There is a slight advantage to an anticlockwise route (6%).	There is no clear advantage either way.
Sailing clockwise	◆ A shorter distance than the anti-clockwise route to enjoy the best months in Scotland. ◆ You will pass the S coast during the off peak season. ◆ Early spring often sees a high pressure system in control over central and NE Europe, when E to NE winds may persist for several days, occasionally lasting 2–3 weeks.	You will pass the S coast during the off peak season.	You will arrive early in the W coast of Scotland – in mid May. Whereas on an anticlockwise route you might not arrive until mid June.
Sailing anticlockwise	See general advantages on page 15 under heading Clockwise v anticlockwise.	The higher up the E coast you start, the less distance you have to travel to the W coast of Scotland to arrive in time for the best months.	Nearly 50% chance of a favourable wind along the S coast in July.

*Calculated assuming the average cruise starting in May and taking 90 days for round Britain. The wind direction information was taken from the *Atlantic Routing Charts*.

For a UK and Ireland circumnavigation, most of the factors are the same as round Britain, given that the time frame for cruising is similar. These factors require additional consideration:

➤ *Prevailing wind* There was a marginal advantage of 1-2 per cent for clockwise circumnavigations for both east and south coast starting points, but this is so low that it is statistically not significant. For the west coast, there is no advantage either way.

➤ *Swell* The Atlantic swell on the exposed coasts of Ireland has a big impact on your trip. The size of the swell at times will prevent you from leaving harbour. From June onwards the onshore winds are more frequent and the chances of a large swell increase.

Does the start date affect your route?

In theory, in an average year, you are likely to encounter more headwinds the later you set off whatever way you go:

Clockwise route The later you set off, the more established the westerly and south-westerly winds will be on the south coast and so you are likely to experience head winds once you have passed Dover.

Anticlockwise route By August, south-westerly and westerly winds are well established on the west coast and Irish Sea, with the occurrence being around 40 per cent for the quarter and 52 per cent including southerly winds. Therefore, passing through the Irish Sea before August should reduce your chances of meeting adverse winds. However, you may just be lucky and pick up a wind with a northerly element.

The experiences of other circumnavigators
Yachts

Let's now look at the actual experience of the yachtsmen who have completed a circumnavigation and see how much motoring was involved.

Based on starting point Most people on the south coast go clockwise. Whereas for those on the east coast, the decision is split, though seven of the nine boats that went clockwise started from Woodbridge or further south. The percentage of time spent sailing is similar, regardless of starting point or direction traveled, which supports the theoretical prediction.

Based on route Looking at the direction based on route provided little insight, with the exception of UK and Ireland, where five out of six boats travelled clockwise regardless of their starting point.

	Most popular direction	Clockwise		Anticlockwise	
		Number of yachts	Percentage sailing hours (of total)	Number of yachts	Percentage sailing hours (of total)
East coast	Anticlockwise	9	49% (7)	10	46% (6)
South coast	Clockwise	20	51% (13)	7	46% (5)
West coast	Clockwise	1	90% (1)		

Note: not all yachts were able to provide the information to calculate the percentage time sailing, hence the sample size is in brackets

Motorboats and RIBs
It is difficult to draw conclusions with so little data but it would appear that anticlockwise is the favoured direction for motorboats and clockwise for RIBs.

	Boat	Most popular direction	Clockwise number of boats	Anticlockwise number of boats
East coast	Motor	Anticlockwise	0	2
South coast	Motor	Anticlockwise	3	5
	RIB	Clockwise	2	1
West coast	Motor	Clockwise	1	

Our trip
With a start date of 1 May, we picked a clockwise route to benefit from the better weather on the west coast of Scotland in June. We were hoping for the prevailing SW up the west coast of the UK, but didn't really pick it up until after the Crinan Canal. Yet on the way down the east coast, we met headwinds, or a lack of wind, for much of the way. This meant that we were motor sailing for quite a lot of the time. This was frustrating and we thought it was perhaps just us, until we met a couple on a Beneteau, who expressed the same frustration. The surveys showed that this was a common experience; the average time spent motoring or motor sailing of the total hours taken, was 54 per cent.

We came back believing that anticlockwise would have been a better direction. But one other skipper who went anticlockwise from the same starting point, at the same time of year wished they had gone clockwise. When researching this book I thought that I would find the right answer, either from my research or the surveys. However, I have come to the conclusion there is no one right answer because there are so many variables – some unpredictable, some conflicting and some that you may be able to overcome by taking on extra crew. So you need to make the decision based on the factors that are important to you.

CREW

You may need to take on additional crew for certain legs or all the way around. This should be considered in your route planning. John Hill (*Almacantar*, Hustler 38), who completed a successful round Britain via Cape Wrath in 2005, broke his trip up into nine fixed legs, with different crew on each leg. His voyage involved 44 crew, which was quite a logistical exercise to organise, but he only had two crew members drop out before the start. His advice for organising the crew:

➤ Only use people you know and have sailed with before, or crew that have been recommended by other skippers.
➤ Try to balance crews so that you have a group with differing depths of experience on each leg.
➤ Ensure that you have a mate who can cope without you if necessary.
➤ Put everything in writing to ensure a commitment; this also gives you a chance to sell the adventure to them.
➤ Try to arrange for the mate to arrive before the rest of the crew to help with the preparations.
➤ Put them in touch with each other and let them sort out their own transport arrangements such as National Express Coaches – a very economical way to travel.
➤ Try to match the crews to the sailing conditions, ie stronger crews for more challenging parts such as the Irish Sea.
➤ Give all crew a briefing on house and safety rules when they arrive on board.
➤ Give them an easy first day, if possible.
➤ Keep them well fed and watered.
➤ Share the work.
➤ Allow a few days at each changeover point to allow for arrivals and departures and so everyone can recharge their batteries.

John's aim was *not* to make a profit on the expenses:

➤ *Food* He charged each person a fixed fee of £5 per day for food.
➤ *Drink* He kept a sheet on the bulkhead recording what had been drunk and charged a fixed fee of 50p for lager; £1 for beer and £5 for a bottle of wine; he then simply shared the total between the numbers onboard.
➤ *Harbour charges* He kept a record of harbour charges etc and divided it between everyone.

John had fixed change-over points, which can reduce the flexibility of your schedule. So you might prefer to have variable ones. The advice from David and Mary Trim (*Jemima* Onvi 385) on variable changeovers is to make sure that your crew know that getting to the boat will be the challenging bit. Their joining instructions read: 'Reaching *Jemima* will probably be the biggest challenge of the trip. As we are uncertain of exact locations, we suggest that you contact us one week before your date of arrival to get an idea of where the sailing party will be. We will then stay in touch over the course of the following week and be able to give you a precise location two to three days beforehand. You will need to be patient and maintain a sense of humour during this time, which will be rewarded on arrival!'

CHARTERING A BOAT AND SKIPPER

If you don't own a boat, it is possible to complete this trip by chartering one. Charterers David and Mary Trim gave me some advice for making a success of this arrangement:

➤ Go on a taster trip and then ensure that the skipper wants to do it for his own reasons, so check his motivation.

➤ Work with a named skipper; eight weeks or however many you have arranged, is a long time, so you need to know the person and be comfortable with them.

➤ Decide what you can afford and mould the programme around the number of weeks you can pay for.

➤ Be clear about what's included and what will cost extra. Be very clear about the initial deposit/final payment amounts and dates due.

➤ Draft a proposal very early on, with objectives and key areas as a basis for shaping an expedition agreement.

➤ Keep in regular touch with the chartering company; appoint one person who is able to make all financial decisions and co-ordinate planning of the route.

➤ Arrange cancellation insurance very early.

➤ During the trip, have a weekly meeting to review how it is going; this can be an opportunity for raising issues.

➤ Recognise the roles. The skipper is in charge. The charterer has responsibilities too, such as paying for marina fees etc. If some crew members have short fuses, and you recognise potential personality clashes, either limit their participation or make sure the overall makeup of crew can handle it.

➤ Decide who is going to do the catering on board. If it is to be shared, make sure this is known in advance.

➤ Make a very clear business plan for the costs. The Trim's trip was based on a charter rate which covered up to four crew. This was less than the cost of two places on another scheme, plus they had a better skipper and boat, albeit shorter in time than the other 12 or 13-week schemes on offer.

ROUTE PLANNING
Schedule

Most people need to be back at their home port by a certain date, therefore it is important to have a rough schedule, so you can determine whether you are ahead or behind your plan. It helps to break the trip into legs, then you can plan how much time to spend in each area. Our split was:

Month 1	Gosport to Campbeltown
Month 2	Campbeltown to Orkneys
Month 3	Orkneys to Whitby
Month 4	Whitby to Gosport

We only spent about 25 per cent (one month) on the west coast of Scotland; this was not enough time. If I was to repeat this trip, I would plan to spend at least six weeks (approximately 40 per cent) on the west coast of Scotland as there is so much to see. Certainly, most of the sailors who contributed to the survey said that the west coast was one of the many highlights of the trip. One couple successfully completed an anticlockwise trip in eight weeks via the Caledonian Canal. Interestingly, they didn't head south after leaving the Canal, they turned right and cruised around the Inner Hebrides visiting Canna, Skye, Rum, Staffa, Iona and Jura. For anyone considering a Caledonian route, if time allows, I would strongly suggest this, otherwise you will miss out on some stunningly beautiful cruising.

Next, you need to work out which ports you want to visit, taking into account the draft of your vessel, using pilot books. To build a realistic plan, you must allow for rest days after long passages, bad weather and work days. This will give you a rough idea of your timing. Sometimes you will be ahead of your schedule and sometimes behind. If you are behind, you may need to do longer legs to catch up. The spare days also allow you to catch up on your chores: washing, shopping etc which always take longer without a washing machine and a car.

Sailing towards the Small Isles

Yachts On average yachts spent 58 per cent of their days at sea, therefore every week you need to plan two spare days. However, if planning a single-handed trip, give yourself more time for recovery.

Number on board (number sampled)	Percentage days at sea	Average cruise duration (days)
1 (12)	50%	106
2 (21)	55%	95
3 (7)	62%	75
4–5 (6)	75%	69
6 + (2)	87%	54

Motorboats If you are in a motor boat you can cover the distance more quickly but you should still allow spare days, as the weather conditions will restrict you more than if you were sailing. On average the motorboats spent 64 per cent of their days at sea and RIBs spent 76 per cent.

THE ROUTE

For the purposes of describing the route I am assuming here a clockwise circumnavigation starting at Penzance. The four extremities (most northerly etc) of your circumnavigation will provide key milestones and you will pass each with a real sense of achievement. These are Dunnet Head (north), Lowestoft Ness (east), Lizard Point (south) and Ardnamurchan Point (west). Those on mainland Britain and Ireland are shown on the map (right). The Dingle Peninsula is Europe's most westerly point. Stotfield Head is less well known but will be the most northerly point if passing through the Caledonian Canal. Two other important milestones are Land's End and Cape Wrath.

You now have the difficult task of deciding what harbours and anchorages to visit. Following my survey, I have looked at the most common routes and the places that were recommended by other circumnavigators.

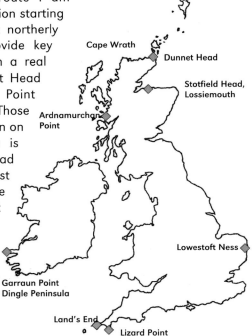

Cape Wrath

Dunnet Head

Stotfield Head, Lossiemouth

Ardnamurchan Point

Lowestoft Ness

Garraun Point
Dingle Peninsula

Land's End

Lizard Point

Catching the Tide
10th May – Penzance to Padstow

Alarm went off at 2:15am and I dragged myself out of bed. Mags was already whirling round the boat making lunch, disconnecting shore power etc, while I was struggling to function at this hour. Up on deck I noticed that there was no sign of the lock keeper and the lock was still closed. 'Great, I can go back to bed and blame the absent lock keeper for delaying our trip.' But within seconds he saw me and asked if we were ready and offered to open the lock gate. 'Damn', I thought, 'no more sleep'. We left the harbour at 3am and we were on our way.

Planning this leg was quite tricky as there are 3 tidal gates. One at the start (the lock opening), one at Land's End and a bar to get over at Padstow – most of which is sand when the tide is out. It was impossible to meet all three, so we had to push against the tide round Land's End. The early start was rewarded with the most spectacular sunrise over the cliffs at Land's End. We rounded Longship lighthouse, marking some rather unfriendly rocks and started to head north for the first time.

We carried on motoring, using the mainsail as a steadying sail (as there is always an Atlantic swell, even on a calm day), and I went off watch – we tended to sleep 3 hours on, 3 hours off on long trips. Fog came in and visibility was between half and one mile. Mags fired up the electronic aids: radar etc and began tracking any targets and the coast. This meant that entering Padstow harbour was less stressful than if we had been navigating without electronics.

**The River Camel (looking out towards the Doom Bar)
with Padstow nestled on the left**

Ituna anchored in Puilladobhrain

PENZANCE TO ST DAVID'S HEAD VIA LIZARD POINT
(mainland Britain most southerly point)

General description of the area

There are relatively long legs (a couple between 70-80nm) and careful timing is needed to make the tidal gates.

Dramatic rugged cliffs fringe the coast of Cornwall. Once round Land's End you are exposed to the Atlantic swell. North Cornwall has few useable harbours unless you can take the ground. The Pembrokeshire coast, with its warm red tones, is memorable and there is much bird life around the volcanic islands of Skomer and Grassholme.

If you have fine weather, try to visit the Isles of Scilly or Lundy.

Standard cruising route	Penzance/Newlyn – Padstow – Milford Haven/Dale – Fishguard/Arklow
Don't miss	*Isles of Scilly* – in particular New Grimsby Sand. You can anchor in crystal clear turquoise waters with white sand. *Padstow* This is an attractive locked harbour.
Major tidal gates	The Lizard, Lands End, Doom Bar, Bishops and Clerks or Ramsey and Jack Sound, depending on your route inside or outside the islands off the Pembrokeshire Coast.

Ituna in Padstow (centre boat)

WEST COAST OF IRELAND: CROSSHAVEN TO PORTRUSH
via Garraun Point, Dingle Peninsula (mainland Ireland's most westerly point)

General description of the area

It is approximately 42nm across St Georges Channel from Wales to Wexford and 140nm from the Isles of Scilly.

On the exposed west coast, you will encounter the long rolling Atlantic swell. When it meets the reflected wave from the coast, it can cause quite disturbed seas. There are many headlands where the weather can hold you up in their lee. The north coast is also exposed to the swell in westerly and northerly winds.

Secure harbours are located at convenient intervals (with a couple of exceptions eg west coast of County Clare) with a comprehensive network of marinas, public moorings and anchorages. Deep water around southern and western coasts of Ireland means that the majority of harbours are accessible at any state of the tide. However, whilst they provide shelter, many harbours on the west coast are unsafe to enter in very bad weather.

Kinsale to Dingle is Ireland's most popular cruising ground, with impressive coastal scenery. Beautiful anchorages can be found in the rias which are deep drowned rivers caused by changes in sea levels. The west coast has miles of raw, natural beauty interspersed with tiny, quaint villages. The wild and dramatic Connemara mountains provide a stunning backdrop to anchorages and harbours on the Galway coast. Donegal is the remotest and least visited part of Ireland's coastline but you are rewarded with a spectacularly varied coastline: deserted beaches, turquoise waters and rugged cliffs.

Useful website: www.sailing.ie/cruising/marinas.asp.

Standard cruising route	*Crosshaven* is the usual arrival point if departing from the Isles of Scilly and *Waterford* if leaving the south Welsh coast. Crosshaven – Kinsale – Glandore – Baltimore – Bantry Bay (Bere Island/ Lawrence Cove/Glengarriff) – Sneem/ Derryname/Valentia – Dingle – Scraggane Bay/Fenit/ Carrigaholt – Kilronan – Roundstone/ Clifden – Inishbofin – Blacksod – Broad Haven – Killybegs/Teelin – Aranmore – Tory Island/Sheephaven – Lough Swilly (Portsalon/ Rathmullan/Denree Head) – Portrush
Don't miss	There are many memorable anchorages and harbours including: *Historic Kinsale* – known as Ireland's gourmet capital. *Picturesque Glandore*, Glengarriff (Bantry Bay). *Sneem* in the Kenmare River. *The Skelligs* and the beehive huts. *Blasket Islands*, Ireland's equivalent of St Kilda.

	Dingle harbour (get escorted in by Fungi, the resident dolphin and unofficial harbour master). *Aran Islands* (Galway Bay) – home of the famous sweaters. *The Roses*, pink granite rocks which are sheltered by a string of islands, similar to those in north Brittany. *Mulroy Bay* has some of the finest Irish scenery.
Major tidal gates	The many prominent headlands: Mizen Head, Valentia, Loop Head, Slyne Head, Ennis Head, Rossan Point and Malin Head and the sounds between the islands and the mainland eg Dursey Sound, Blasket Sound. Tides are approximately 1–2kt on south and west; close to headlands they can reach 4kt.
Events	Cork week in mid July.

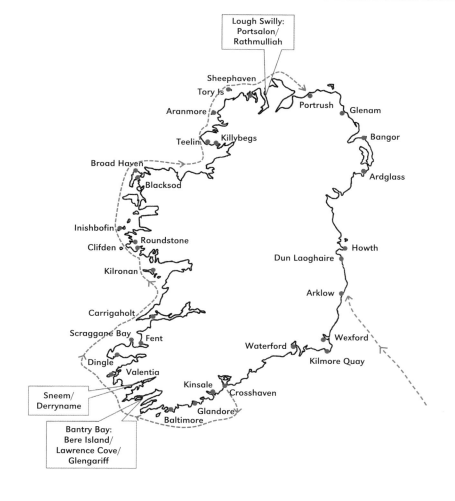

PASSAGE THROUGH THE IRISH SEA

General description of the area

If you get good weather to explore the Welsh coast, you will find variety – from popular resorts with sandy beaches to lush green hills and wooded banks; parts of the coast have the Welsh hills or mountains as their backdrop. However, Cardigan Bay can be a dangerous lee shore in strong onshore winds, with little refuge to be gained from the harbours along the coast due to the bars that guard their entrances. The coast of Ireland may provide a safer passage in strong south-westerlies. The east coast provides contrast from cities to small towns and villages; rolling hills give way to sheer cliffs as you go north towards Ballycastle.

The Isle of Man is a very useful refuge in the middle of the Irish Sea. The Solway Firth is a beautiful area but has hazardous sandbanks that east coast sailors would be proud of. Only Kirkcudbright is suitable for visitors to the area but it is worth a visit. Only 20 miles separates Ireland from Scotland across the North Channel.

Standard cruising route	Fishguard – Holyhead – Isle of Man – Portpatrick – Campbeltown Milford Haven – Arklow – Dun Laoghaire/Howth – Ardglass – Bangor – Glenarm If crossing to explore the east coast of Ireland, it is usually from Milford Haven or the Isle of Man. If you are planning to go round the Mull of Kintyre, the north Antrim coast is a popular route, leaving from Glenarm or Ballycastle to avoid the challenges of the tides close to the Mull.
Don't miss	*Ardglass* – a small and homely harbour. *Strangford Lough* – beautiful and completely sheltered. *Howth* – a pleasant setting with access to Dublin. *Kirkcudbright* – gentle scenic beauty.
Major tidal gates	At springs there are 4kt through St George's Channel and 5kt through the North Channel. *Wales*: Bardsey Sound, Menai Straits and South Stack. *IOM*: Calf Sound, *SW Scotland*: Mull of Galloway, *N Ireland*: Torr Head and Fair Head.

Campbeltown

South Stack

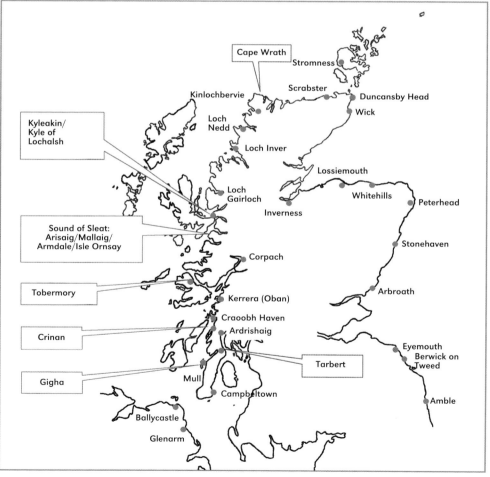

NORTH-WEST SCOTLAND:
MULL OF KINTYRE TO ARDNAMURCHAN POINT

General description of the area

You will do short day passages, with only short hops across open sea. Unless you get bad weather, you will rarely lose sight of land. Navigation is mainly by eye; ensure that the chart matches the land and use transits and clearing bearings. Whichever way you look when you are sailing, there is a stunning view.

Firth of Clyde: Many people on a round-Britain cruise don't have time to visit the beautiful cruising ground of Lochs Long and Fyne, and the Kyles of Bute.

You will pass the southern isles of Gigha, Islay and Jura if you round the Mull – the later two will give you an opportunity to sample a 'wee dram' from their distilleries.

Puilladobhrain (pronounced 'Pull door en' and means 'pool of the otter') was our favourite (see photo on page 24). We were lucky to share it with only one other boat on a sunny day; there was scarcely a ripple on the sea and while anchored there we saw the most spectacular sunset over Mull.

Although you may plan to go on the standard route, I do recommend that you take advantage of this spectacular cruising ground.

Tarbert Loch Fyne en route to the Crinan Canal

Standard cruising route	Glenarm/Ballycastle – Gigha – Craobh Haven – Kerrera – Tobermory or Campbeltown – Tarbert - Crinan - Kerrera – Tobermory
Don't miss	Lovely bays and harbours are too numerous to mention but here are a few: *Ardminish Bay (Gigha)* – a peaceful island benefiting from the Gulf stream. *Puilladobhrain (Seil Island)* *Tinkers Hole (Erraid off Mull)* – isolated rock amphitheatre with white sandy sea bed. *West Loch Tarbert (Jura)* – tranquillity and peace. *Tarbert (Loch Fyne)* – picturesque fishing village. *Ardinamir (pronounced 'Ard-nammer') (Luing)* *Gometra Harbour (Ulva/Gometra)* – you can take a boat trip from Ulva to Fingals Cave (Staffa). *Bull Hole* (Mull). *Ardtornish Bay (Loch Aline), Tobermory (Mull)* – a colourful harbour that gets a lot of tourism, partly due to the BBC's Balamory.
Major tidal gates	Mull of Kintyre, Dorus Mor can run up to 8kt. Sound of Mull, Sound of Luing, Cuan Sound, Ardnamurchan Point.
Events	Tarbert Bell Lawrie Series, Scotland's equivalent of Cowes – last week in May.

Tobermory with its colourful quayside houses

NORTHERN SCOTLAND: ARDNAMURCHAN POINT
(most westerly point on mainland Britain) TO CAPE WRATH

General description of the area

You will make short day passages until you pass the Inner Sound. When you enter the Minch you start to experience more open water and pass some major headlands. The Outer Hebrides protects the coast from the Atlantic swell until you reach the top of the Minch. But heavy seas can quickly build up on the exposed headlands. There is a lack of navigational aids and many harbours are unlit, but as the nights are long it is unlikely that you will sail in the dark. Given the tidal streams of the area, transit lines are very useful.

The raw, awe-inspiring scenery of the west coast is almost beyond adequate description. Its scale, depth and remoteness are best appreciated from the sea.

Outer Hebrides: to explore the west coast you will need some settled weather; the same applies to St Kilda, some 40nm to the west. The beaches of South Harris are incredible: white sand with turquoise waters.

The mountains of Loch Torridon

Standard cruising route	Sound of Sleat (pronounced 'Slate') (Arisaig/Mallaig/Armdale/Isle Ornsay) – Kyleakin/Kyle of Lochalsh – Loch Gairloch (Flowerdale/ Shieldaig/Badachro) – Lochinver – Kinlochbervie
Don't miss	Again lovely stopping places are too numerous to mention but include: *Canna Harbour (Canna)* – green and fertile. *Loch Scavaig (Skye)* – one of the most spectacular lochs on the west coast lies under the ridge of the Cuillins – squalls can be equally impressive. *Inverie Bay* (Loch Nevis). *Plockton (Loch Carron)* – an attractive village in a bay surrounded by a bowl of hills; it has such a mild climate that palm trees grow there. *Acarsaid Mor (South Rona)* – a place offering total isolation, apart from seals – once you anchor there, you won't want to leave. *Poll Dhomaine (Inner Sound)* and *Loch a'Chadh-fi* (Loch Laxford) – remote anchorages. *Vatersay (Barra)* – white beach and turquoise waters. *Eilean Hingerstay (Lewis)* – remote and intimate.
Major tidal gates	Kyle Rhea (6 to 8kt at springs); Rubha Reidh, Stoerhead, Cape Wrath.

Grobust Beach, Westray

NORTHERN SCOTLAND AND NORTHERN ISLES:
Cape Wrath to Wick

General description of the area

The long leg to Orkney or Scrabster is made easier by the light nights.

Vast areas of land are totally uninhabited; and it is much easier to access many of these areas from the sea than by road. If conditions allow, pass close by Sandwood Bay, a 2km deserted sandy beach near to Cape Wrath; it is a 6km hike to see it by land. Rounding Cape Wrath is a big milestone and you have a feeling of being a long way from civilisation. The top north-west corner near Cape Wrath is isolated; you get the feeling that many of the communities are on the edge of survival, following the demise of the fishing industry. You expect the Orkneys to be the same, yet they are vibrant Islands, with a real buzz and feel of a community in control of their destiny. The clarity of the light, the lush vegetation, the turquoise colour of the water and the white sandy beaches, make a cruise around the Orkneys memorable. Although the tides are tricky, good planning, and a healthy respect for them, will ensure safe passage. Their rich history , spanning thousands of years, make a stay very rewarding and if time and money permit, it is worth hiring a car to explore mainland Orkney.

Not many cruisers make it to the Shetlands on this cruise, but a few make the 46nm passage from Westray to Fair Isle. You will meet quite a few yachts en route to and from Norway.

Standard cruising route	Kinlochbervie – Stromness – Scapa Flow – Wick or Kinlochbervie – Scrabster – Wick or Kinlochbervie – Stromness – Kirkwall – Wick
Don't miss	*Kinlochbervie* – fish and chips at the Fishermen's mission. *Kyle of Tongue.* *Orkney* – Italian Chapel, Skara Brae *Westray* – the puffins, Grobust Beach and the friendly harbour master.
Major tidal gates	Cape Wrath; the whole of the Orkney Islands. In particular: Eyenhallow Sound, Westray Firth, Hoy Sound and the Pentland Firth.
Events	Orkney Music festival: mid June.

Mainland Orkney

NORTH-EAST SCOTLAND:
Wick to Eyemouth

General description of the area

The east coast of Scotland is far more exposed and there are few natural harbours, so most are man-made and are accessed by skinny entrances. This gives you an indication of the power of the seas in the winter months along this coast. Have a look at the picture in the harbour master's office in Whitehills if you want to see evidence! Reasonable weather is required to enter many of the ports along this coast. So if the weather turns bad, you will either be storm-bound or end up making long passages.

Most harbours were created in the prosperous days of herring fishing, the 'silver darlings'. The active fishing fleet is now concentrated into a few harbours, where pleasure boats are often none too welcome. Eyemouth is one exception; it is a busy fishing port, but very welcoming to all.

The scenery is varied: from the fortress-like cliffs of Sutherland to the golden sands and pine-clad coastline of the Moray Firth. From Wick/Helmsdale, there is always the temptation to cut in a straight line across to Whitehills or Peterhead – though you miss out on the beautiful Moray Firth.

The Firth of Forth offers many pretty fishing harbours, though in many places you need to take the ground.

Standard cruising route	Wick – Whitehills – Peterhead – Stonehaven – Arbroath – Eyemouth

The busy and friendly fishing port of Eyemouth. We were relieved to see there are still some fishing boats left in the UK

Don't miss	*Caledonian Canal* – mooring off Urquhart Castle. *Lossiemouth* – ice cream; cruising across Spey Bay. *Stonehaven* – a charming harbour.
Major tidal gates	Chanonry Narrows (from the Caledonian Canal), Rattray Head.
Events	Port Soy: traditional boat weekend in July.

Top: The skinny harbour entrance at Whitehills. There is a sharp 90 degree corner at the end of a narrow entrance

Right: *Ituna* moored against the outside harbour wall at Stonehaven, which is only tenable in good weather

EASTERN ENGLAND: BERWICK UPON TWEED TO DOVER
via Lowestoft (Britain's most easterly point)

General description of the area

Northumberland's coastline is memorable with its castles, wild sandy beaches and islands. As you sail south, the landscape becomes more industrial until you get to the Yorkshire moors. Whilst there is no shortage of harbours along this coast, some have tidal restrictions such as Hartlepool, Amble and Whitby. Whitby is very atmospheric, particularly in the early morning before the tourists emerge.

The Humber is characterised by sand banks, strong tides, shipping and gas rigs. Spurn Point makes a useful overnight stay and prevents a long haul up to the Humber marinas, which are governed by locks and so accessible only at certain times of the day. At this point, the chart changes colour, as sandbanks appear everywhere. You have to wind your way through the maze of sandbanks, gats and swatch ways.

Wells-next-the-Sea is a beautiful tidal harbour but you need local knowledge (available from the welcoming harbour master) to enter, due to the shifting sands. Like many harbours on this part of the coast, entry is only safe in good weather.

East coast river cruising is a delight – a different pace of life. If you are lucky you may see a Thames barge in full sail. If you have time, a trip up to London is an experience.

Standard cruising route	Eyemouth – Amble – Blyth – Hartlepool – Whitby – Scarborough/ Bridlington/Spurn Head – Wells – Lowestoft – River Orwell (Harwich/Shotley) – Ramsgate – Dover. Those choosing not to dry out miss out Bridlington and Wells.
Don't miss	*Holy Island or The Kettle (Farne Islands)* – there is an abundance of wildlife including puffins and seals. *Newcastle* – moor up at the pontoon by the blinking eye bridge. *Amble Marina* – the bath! *Southwold* – river mooring; great fish and chips at the Harbour Inn. *Pin Mill (River Orwell)* – the majestic old Thames barges. *Walton Backwaters* – Arthur Ransome fans will know this as Secret Water. *Pyefleet Creek* (River Blackwater) – idyllic anchorage. Sailing up to Pin Mill
Major tidal gates	The Norfolk coast and the Goodwin Sands.

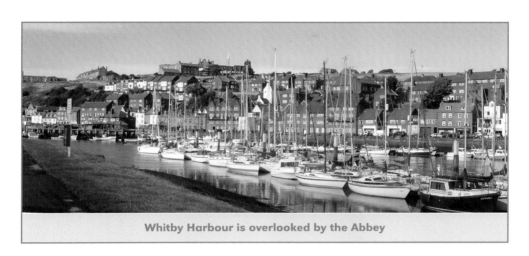

Whitby Harbour is overlooked by the Abbey

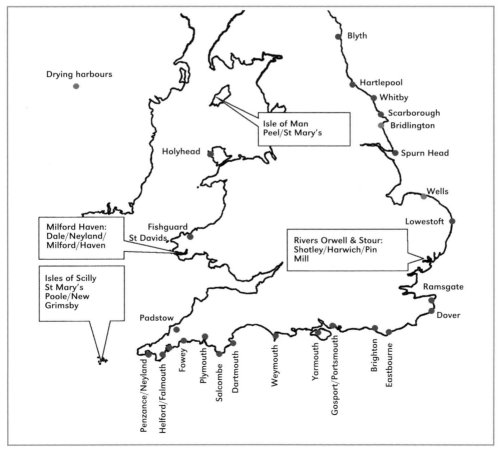

SOUTHERN ENGLAND: DOVER TO LAND'S END
(via the Lizard – Britain's most southerly point)

General description of the area

As you head west, the harbour dues increase dramatically. Don't be surprised when the daily harbour fee can be the equivalent of a week's fee elsewhere.

Dover is tucked into the base of the impressive White Cliffs; these chalk cliffs will be visible along much of the south coast, all the way along to the Jurassic Dorset coast.

The naval history is evident immediately as you enter the Solent with the impressive Napoleonic Forts and the invisible (but very hard) submarine barrier. If you can, avoid visiting the Solent during the weekend, so you can sample the delights of Newtown Creek, Beaulieu or Yarmouth without seeing masses of other boats and tourists. The historic ships in Portsmouth are worth a visit.

Once you pass the Needles, the boating density drops considerably. The natural harbour of Poole provides both peaceful anchorages and good facilities in the marinas. There are many charming harbours and anchorages in the west country.

Standard cruising route	Dover – Eastbourne – Brighton – Portsmouth – Yarmouth (Isle of Wight) – Weymouth – Dartmouth – Salcombe – Plymouth – Fowey – Falmouth – Helford
Don't miss	*Chichester Harbour* – a peaceful natural harbour. *Beaulieu* – a winding river which will take you back in time. *Studland or Worbarrow Bay.* *Dartmouth* – spectacular entry between the forts. *Newton Ferriers* – a peaceful Devon village. *Fowey* – a busy Cornish town with steep, narrow streets. *Helford Passage* – the wooded Cornish river which has creeks that have inspired many writers.
Major tidal gates	Beachy Head, the Needles, Portland Bill and Start Point.
Events	Cowes week: first week in August. It is a very popular event so expect to raft five deep.

THE CANALS

As well as providing short cuts, canals provide a break, slowing down the pace and allowing you time to relax and enjoy the scenery. Remember that the canals are fresh water, so you need to allow for the increase of your draft by 10cm. Though the depths of the canals may vary from the minimum depth stated, so it is always advisable to phone ahead to the sea lock keepers to confirm. The entry and exit from the sea locks are constrained by the time of the tides.

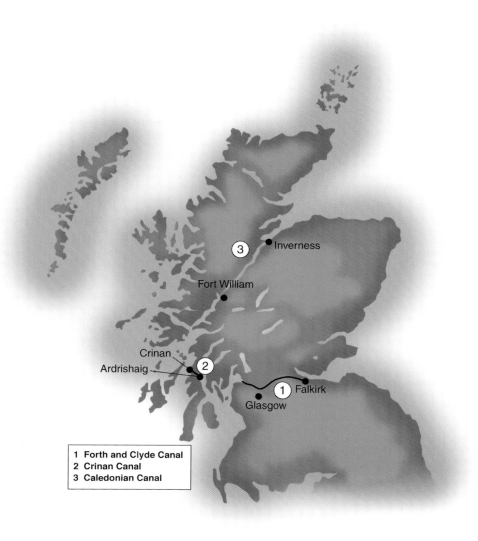

1 Forth and Clyde Canal
2 Crinan Canal
3 Caledonian Canal

Forth and Clyde Canal

This restored canal, reopened for use in 2001, connects the Firths of Clyde and Forth. This route takes you through large towns with busy areas and also peaceful country-side and passes the Falkirk wheel, the first rotating boat lift.

Details	Statistics
Length	31 nm
Number of locks	39
Number of self-operated locks	Most of them
Depth of water	1.83m (3ft 6in)
Width of channel	3.5m (11ft 6in)
Max height	2.7m (8ft 10in) – yachts have to demast at Bowling, Port Edgar or at contractors along the River Carron. The service is included in the licence fee for Bowling – but there is a charge at the Eastern end between £29–£40 depending on boat length (2008).
Length due to locks/wheel	19.2m (70ft)
Opening hours	0800 – 1800 during daylight hours, though you need to book passage in advance.
Licences	£6 per metre for a 5-day licence (2008). For up-to-date details, phone 01324 483034
Transit time	A minimum of 24 hours including the passage from Port Edgar and the negotiation of the River Carron to the sea lock. This excludes unstepping and resteppping the mast.

One boat in the survey took three days to transit the canal: two nights in the canal and one night at Grangemouth, though it could have been completed quicker. You can only pass under the new road bridge at certain times, so it may mean an early start.

Loch Lochy forms part of the Caledonian Canal (pages 44–5), which locks at Gairlochy. Photo: David and Mary Trim

Crinan Canal

Described as Scotland's prettiest short cut, it meanders the short distance from Ardrishaig (pronounced 'r–drish –ig') at the north-west extremity of the Clyde across mid Argyll to emerge at Crinan. It allows you to miss out the Mull of Kintyre, which has strong tides; if you look at the weather for Malin Head (graph 2, page 12), just across the water from the Mull, you will see that it can be stormy in the summer.

Details	Statistics
Length	14.5km
Number of locks	15 locks and 7 bridges
Number of operated locks	3 and main road bridges
Number of self-operated locks	12
Depth of water	2.89m (9ft 6in)
Width of channel	6.09m (20ft)
Max height	28.95m (95ft)
Length due to locks/wheel	26.82m (88ft)
Opening hours	7 days per week
Licences	£9.70 (2008) per metre for a 3-day licence; this gives you berthing free of charge. For up-to-date details, phone 01546 603210
Transit time	A minimum of half a day. The average transit time of the 14 boats surveyed passing through the Crinan was 1.7 days.

You can pre-arrange for assistance for the 12 hand-operated locks at the sea locks. In 2006, it cost us £40 for lock keeper Hugh's help and it was money well spent. He opened all the locks in advance and he was there to take our lines; plus we got information about the canal. It is a good option if you are short-handed. At busy times, book well in advance.

Hugh, the lock keeper (right), closing a lock on the Crinan Canal

Caledonian Canal

The natural feature, known as the Great Glen Fault, divides the Highlands, running from Inverness to Fort William and follows a 60 mile fissure scoured out by glaciers during the last ice age. During the Jacobite rebellions, the Glen had great strategic importance in controlling the Highland clans, enforced through the presence of forts at Fort William, Fort Augustus and Fort George, at the mouth of the Moray Firth.

Joining up the lochs of the Great Glen, was considered as early as 1726 but work did not start until 1803. It was a huge undertaking, as the 22 miles of man-made canal were cut using only picks, shovels and muscle power. Designed by Thomas Telford, it was Britain's first state-funded transport project taking 19 years to build at a cost of £840,000 and opening in 1822. However, it was not a commercial success as at 14 feet deep, it was too shallow to take large shipping. It was only deepened, to Telford's original plans of 20ft (6m), 25 years later. The concept of the canal was not just to create employment and revitalise the Highlands but it was also designed to be a short cut, missing out the treachous Pentland Firth. However, by the time the canal was deep enough, sail had given way to steam and the Pentland Firth was not such an obstacle. The canal was used to transport timber and other goods but its use declined from 1880.

The canal climbs 105ft (32m) from sea level and features staircases, flights of interconnected locks, in which the top gates of one lock are the bottom gates of the next. Eight locks make up Neptune's staircase at Banavie just north of Fort William. With Ben Nevis as a backdrop, it is truly spectacular, as it raises vessels 70ft above sea level in a distance of 500yd (21m in 457m). There are two other staircases at Muirtown and Fort Augustus. The staircases were more economical to build, but in practice they created bottlenecks for transiting vessels. Though passage through the canal is more relaxing since the 29 locks were mechanised over 30 years ago. The canal survived because of its importance to the local economy and is still widely used by commercial traffic and leisure craft.

Dramatic scenery

En route, the Caledonian Canal passes dramatic scenery: the Great Lochs of Lochy (photo on page 42) and Oich, the infamous Loch Ness and the historic Urquhart Castle. It offers the opportunity to drop anchor in some tranquil spots and you will pass through Chanonry Narrows at the entrance to the Moray Firth, which is reputedly the best place in the UK to see dolphins.

Anchorages

The 'Caley' is made up of four Lochs, and all bar Loch Dochfour have recommended anchorages. Despite being 752ft (228m) deep, Loch Ness has a few anchorages: at Urquhart Bay, in the shadow of the imposing 13th Century Castle, Dores Bay and Foyers Bay. You can anchor in Loch Oich by the River Garry and Loch Lochy at Anchnacarry Bay and the surrounding bays.

Urquhart castle on the shores of Loch Ness is a beautiful place to stop overnight either on the buoy placed there or in the tiny harbour. Bizarrely it has a 'pay and display' machine for mooring your boat alongside.

Details	Statistics
Length	50nm
Number of locks	29 locks and 10 bridges
Number of operated locks	All
Depth of water	4.11m (13ft 6in)
Width of channel	10.67m (35ft)
Max height	35m (115ft). Note that Kessock Bridge on Inverness Firth is 27.4m (89ft)
Length due to locks/wheel	45.72m (150ft)
Opening hours	7 days per week 0800 – 1800 during the summer months.
Licences	For up-to-date details phone 01463 725500. £16.50 (2008) per metre for an 8-day transit.
Transit time	A minimum of two days. The average transit time of the 13 yachts surveyed passing through the canal, was 3.6 days and 4.3 days for the 3 motorboats surveyed.

CHARTS

Having decided on the places you are going to visit, you can start to work out which charts you need. They are one of the major expenses of the trip, so it is worth choosing them carefully.

Which charts do you need?

Everyone has their preferences when it comes to charts, mine are the Admiralty charts, but given their cost, it would be prohibitively expensive to carry only Admiralty charts. Imray charts proved to be very good value as they included charts of several ports. They tend to be quite small scale, so they are particularly good for long legs and route planning, but for coastal navigation you sometimes need the larger scale available on the Admiralty charts. The leisure folios (from both Imray and the Admiralty) are excellent value. The Admiralty are expanding their range at a folio per quarter and already cover a large portion of the coastline. Increased coverage by the folios will reduce the cost of charts, and since our trip in 2006, 18 of the charts we took have now been replaced by five folios. If you are just passing through an area, it will be cheaper to buy one chart rather than the folio. A free publication, *NP109*, shows all the Admiralty charts of the UK and their scale, so it helps you to see which charts are available.

Your charts need to cover where you are planning to go, your emergency ports, and any alternative routes, for example the Caledonian Canal if you are planning to use it as a potential short cut. You also need to consider the scale of the charts required. We did not use all the charts that we took because some covered places not visited. We carried too many detailed charts. Looking at scale and how we used the charts, I would draw the following conclusions:

Crossing open water When crossing open water we would use the small-scale Imray charts, for example Cardigan Bay (1:145,000) and Irish Sea (1:280,000).

Coastal navigation This varied depending on the nature of the area and the available charts:

- ➤ Navigating close to the land, round sandbanks between islands: the scale ranged from 1:50.000 to 1:100,000.
- ➤ On coasts where the water depth is relatively deep close to the shore, and so without obstacles to surface navigation, we would use the Imray charts which tend to be 1:250000, for example Moray Firth to Dundee (C23) or Admiralty charts 1:200,000.
- ➤ On the west coast of Scotland, when navigating to an anchorage or harbour, or close to rocks, we would use Admiralty charts with a scale of a maximum of 1:25,000.
- ➤ For entering harbours we generally used charts between 1:7500 and 1:15,000. These are included on many of the Imray charts or in leisure folios.

The list of charts we took is in Appendix 1. Membership of the Cruising Association proved invaluable as they have a chart library where I could research the charts that I needed. You need only to reduce your list by a couple of charts to pay for the joining fee. Also they offer 10 per cent discount on all Imray books and charts; this also extends to Admiralty charts that are in the Imray catalogues.

Electronic charts

The type of chart that you can use is determined by your chart plotter. If you are lucky, you will be able to use one cartridge for the whole area. Do make sure you check your electronic charts before you set off; we bought ours new and when we needed the west Scotland cartridge we discovered that it was faulty. It was exchanged with no quibble by Cmap but it was a pain to send it back and arrange for the new one to be delivered. If your electronic charts are updated annually, make sure you buy them *after* the update.

Ardnamurchan Point

3

FINANCES

TAKE POSITIVE ACTION TO MAKE IT HAPPEN

Lack of finance is one reason why people don't go on an extended cruise. So put a financial plan in place to make sure it happens. First calculate how much money you will need. For a short cruise most people will not rent out their house. Therefore, you need to calculate:

➤ The running costs for your house when you are away, including financial commitments, such as the mortgage, utility bills etc. If you leave your house empty, you need to inform your insurance company which may result in a slight increase in the premium.

➤ Pre-trip costs such as charts, pilot books and additional equipment required to prepare the boat.

➤ Cruising costs such as food, fuel and harbour fees.

➤ Any additional costs for your return journey home. If you are returning to employment, remember that most employers pay at the end of the month, so allow for that.

➤ A contingency fund: if you have no guaranteed income on your return, then you will need some cash reserves to live off until you can start earning.

If you find that you don't have enough funds for the trip, then you must take some positive action. The steps we took to make sure our dream became reality were to:

➤ Set up a regular saving scheme 18 months before our start date.
➤ Generate money through eBay. We boosted our cruising budget by £600 through selling old sailing kit; it paid for the electronic charts.

PRE-TRIP COSTS

There are several pre-trip costs:

Boat insurance

Most policies insure from Elbe to Brest, so this will cover your route. Our insurance company didn't charge us any more than our usual annual premium. Clearly you should check this with your insurance company.

Charts and pilot books

Charts are a major cost of the cruise, particularly as you will need quite a number. Our charts cost us:

Item	Cost	Comments
Folios and charts	£1196	We negotiated a 15% discount by buying 5 folios from the Admiralty stand at the London Boat Show. Recently they have offered 25% discount when spending more than £100. ■ 5 Admiralty folios – excludes 4 already owned ■ 60 Admiralty Charts ■ 9 Imray charts We could have reduced the number of charts taken and new folios would have also reduced this cost further.
Electronic charts	£536	NT+ charts (5 areas required). Each new chart cost £139. One was an upgrade. We negotiated 20% discount from CMap. Navtronics and CMap Max now supply a single cartridge for the whole of the UK, though it is chart plotter dependent.
Admiralty Tidal Atlases	£64	We negotiated 19% discount at LBS.
Reeds Almanac	£33	Covers every UK port and harbour.
Pilot books	£145	Six pilot guides: a mixture of Clyde Cruising Club and Imray pilot guides (excludes pilot guides for the south coast as we already owned these). We obtained 10% discount on Imray books from the Cruising Association.
Total	£1974	

Reducing the cost of the charts

There are several ways to reduce the cost of your charts:

Electronic charts If you need several chart areas, you can exchange chart cartridges for less than the cost of a new one. But this involves a logistical exercise of sending off the cartridge, to exchange, which is fine if you can guarantee to be in one place for a while. We decided to buy all the cartridges then sell them on eBay afterwards; we recouped nearly a third of our outlay.

Paper charts You may be lucky enough to be able to borrow charts from friends. If this is not possible, then another way to reduce costs is by buying second-hand charts. Some sources for second-hand charts are:

➤ eBay.
➤ Boating magazine small ads
➤ Marine Chart Services (MCS). You can set up a wish list with them. They will send you the charts at predefined times so that you reduce your postage costs. They sell several types of Admiralty charts (see their website for the latest costs www.chartsales.co.uk or phone 01933 441629), their categories are:
   ✦ Cancelled
   ✦ Second-hand non-corrected
   ✦ Second-hand corrected
   ✦ New. Note that they sell these at full retail price and there are cheaper sources for new charts, for example by buying from the Cruising Association at a discount.

If you are going to purchase second-hand charts, always check independently whether you are buying a current or a cancelled version of the chart. You can check Admiralty charts by looking up the published date on the UK Hydrographic Office (UKHO) website www.ukho.gov.uk/amd/attachments/SNC_chart_listing.pdf. Also, bear in mind that everyone wants to reduce the cost of their charts. So the earlier you place your order, the more second-hand charts you will get but the more updating you will need to do. We placed our wish list with MCS in February, three months prior to leaving. Maybe if we had placed it sooner we would have been able to get more second-hand charts. This was our split of Admiralty charts:

New Admiralty charts	Number	Second-hand Admiralty charts	Number
Standard	32	Updated	11
Leisure series	4	Not updated	8
		Cancelled	5

The Leisure series are cheaper than the standard charts as they are printed on thinner paper. However, after you have used them, they are more difficult to sell on later. We sold charts and tidal atlases on eBay after the trip to try and recoup some of the costs. One way to reduce the cost of charts and pilot books is to return the same way. It might be better to change your goal than not cruise at all. For example, going round Cape Wrath and returning to the west coast via the Caledonian Canal would mean that many of the charts and pilot books could be reused.

Updating charts If you do buy second-hand charts, make sure you update them. All the issuers have good websites which makes this easier, so you no longer have to trawl through Notices to Mariners for corrections. You can enter the chart number on the website and it lists the updates for that chart. This also applies to the folios. Some charts are issued annually, due to the number of changes, so I decided to buy new charts for these areas.

TRIP COSTS

We logged every expense on the trip into categories, so that we would have a clear understanding of how much it would cost us to go cruising in future. So for our four-month cruising period, costs were as follows:

Category	Description	Daily cost	Total trip cost
Engine and heater running costs	This included oil and diesel for both engine and the Webasto heater (Avg 50p per litre)	£4.11	£468.74
Outboard running costs	Fuel	£0.05	£5.98
Paraffin	Used for cooking	£0.15	£15
Food, household items		£8.67	£988.72
General	Miscellaneous items, including medicines	£1.72	£196.11
Showers, washing	Mostly, showers are included in harbour fees. Five stopovers with family and friends enabled us to do laundry. When summer arrived, we could dry clothes outside rather than in a dryer	£0.63	£71.75

Category	Description	Daily cost	Total trip cost
Entertainment	Meals out (mainly fish and chips and lunches) visiting sites/ buildings, puffin tour (essential), teas, and ice creams.	£4.07	£464.18
Chandlery		£0.40	£45.48
Stationary, books and postage	Includes all reading material	£1.02	£115.79
Souvenirs		£2.10	£239.02
Harbour fees		£12.18	£1388
Crinan Canal	Includes £40 for assistance opening the locks and mooring FOC	£1.30	£148.3
Travel whilst ashore	Includes £128 car hire for 3 days in Orkney	£1.66	£189.42
Communications	Vodafone data card and mobile phone costs	£2.68	£305.54
Repairs	Main cost: purchase of a new Raymarine graphic instrument (£416)	£6.81	£775.95
Total		£47.53	£4373.29

As time went on, we learnt how to reduce our costs and adapt to a life as liveaboards on a limited budget. For example, we stopped having lunches ashore and took sandwiches and drinks or ate on the boat.

Harbour fees

Harbour fees are a major cost, and they contributed to a third of our total cruise budget. They can be reduced if you increase the number of nights spent at anchor. We spent only nine nights at anchor, but the highest number of nights at anchor on any cruise surveyed was 33.

In Scotland, various councils run 'rover' tickets allowing you to visit several harbours at a reduced cost. These tickets allow you to either spend two days at one marina or you can stay at two locations, ie a day in each. Various Scottish councils and Orkney marinas run these. A fourteen-day rover ticket in Orkney cost £102; other 48hr tickets we used cost £16 per ticket. *Reeds Almanac* has a lot of information about rover tickets and the prices of overnight stays. Our costs are shown here:

Harbour	Number of nights	Comments
Marinas	51	Average cost £15.23, reduced due to volume discounts in the Orkneys (14 days) and Lowestoft (9 days).
Pontoon	27	Average cost £13.68 – increased due to the cost of Whitby (6 days).
Mooring buoy	13	Average cost £7.30
Wall	11	Average cost £13.39
Anchor	9	Be aware that if you anchor on the south coast, you are likely to be charged. In Scotland, you will not be charged for anchoring, but if you are in a sea loch (open at one end) the owner can charge you for landing your dinghy above HW; in a sound (open at both ends), charges are not allowed.

Fuel costs

Clearly, if you are in a motorboat, your fuel costs will be a major part of your budget. Even in a yacht, your fuel costs will be higher than you might expect. On average over all the routes, the boats surveyed motored or motor sailed for 54 per cent of their time.

Fuel prices varied enormously; it is always worth finding out from the harbour master where the fishing boats or commercial boats fill up. It is often at a different place to where yotties and motorboats refuel and can be cheaper. The cheapest we paid for diesel was 44p per litre, which was 6p per litre under our average in 2006; the cheaper prices were generally to be found in fishing ports: Kirkwall, Tarbert, Campbeltown and Whitby. In some places we were available to get a volume discount when buying quantities over 100 litres. The highest charge we were quoted (but decided not to fill up) was 10p per litre above our average: 60p in Amble. Most marinas charged around 50p to 54p. So we started to phone ahead and plan where we would bunker up. The price comparisons are given in Appendix 5; whilst prices will change, they give you an indication of the relative differences.

In a motorboat, you will be able to get volume discounts. It is also worth researching a local fuel company and arranging a tanker delivery, which can save 5-12p per litre depending on the volume taken. However, be warned that the flow rate from a tanker is faster than from the diesel pumps and could cause a problem, depending on the size of your pipes. So only fill your tank to 90 per cent capacity, so that you don't get a blow-back.

For advice on fuel availability, see page 164.

Repair costs

Our knowledge of mechanics enables us to do basic fault-finding and servicing such as changing oil and fuel filters, impellers, oil, alternator belts. For anything more complex than this and we need to call an engineer. Both time and money can be saved by carrying more spares, see Chapter 14 for details on what we carried. Repairs accounted for 20 per cent of our costs.

RETURNING HOME

It is advisable to leave money in the bank for expenses when returning home such as MOTs, car tax etc. We discovered that we needed to replace the car, an event which we had certainly not planned for!

SPONSORSHIP AND RAISING MONEY FOR CHARITY

The majority of people do not get sponsorship. But if you do, it is more likely to take the form of equipment rather than money, unless it is a donation to a charity. The key question is what is your unique selling point? What makes your story different to anyone else who is completing the trip? It is unlikely that you will be successful unless:

➤ You are an exciting prospect for a company and will gain them media exposure, as in the case of Katie Miller, a young solo sailor raising money for the Ellen MacArthur Trust.
➤ You intend raising money for charity.
➤ You have a connection with the company.

You need to consider what you can offer your sponsor:

➤ *TV time* This is very attractive but you have to have a really exciting story to attract the interest of TV producers.
➤ *Press articles* targeted at an audience that the company wants to attract.
➤ *Advertising space* on the boat or on your web site. This could take the form of a sticker on the hull, advertising on your sail or a logo on your sail cover.

You need to be prepared to write many letters and start well in advance. If you do get sponsorship, you need to work hard. John Hill (*Almacantar*, Hustler 38) who was raising money for the Lincolnshire Air Ambulance recounts: 'As part of the deal for getting sponsorship, I had to arrange substantial publicity and to this end I achieved interviews with local papers at most of the change-over ports. I sent photographs together with the reports I did for each leg, to the staff of the Air Ambulance, who pushed these out, suitably edited, to many other papers. I carried a sail cover advertising the charity and the Company who sponsored me'.

Loch Gairloch which runs rover tickets with other harbours

The couple most successful at raising money for charity that we found were Bill and Anita Miller (*Marika M* Westerly Corsair). They raised an amazing £14,000 for Stroke Research in 2005 by their cruise round Britain via Cape Wrath. Bill and Anita wrote approximately 250 letters to friends, business contacts and a few companies. They had responses from about 175. Bill suffered a stroke in 1999 and was in a wheelchair for a year which, as Bill says: 'it helped no end' in securing donations. That was his unique story. Often the charities you are supporting are able to help with publicity. Other sources for contributions are:

➤ *Friends and family* Probably the easiest solution for managing your donations is by using the website www.justgiving.com where you will find details of how to set up an account.
➤ *Harbour masters* Mention the charity to the harbour master when you arrive in harbour: he may waive the fees as a donation to your charity, especially if you are raising money for the RNLI.
➤ *Your home marina or harbour* Bill found that his marina waived 50 per cent of their fee, which went into the pot.

The other advantage for a charity is the contribution to raising awareness. Whilst the trip itself might not instantly generate returns, with a raised profile the charity could pick up money in the future in the form of bequests.

4

PREPARATIONS

If you don't plan preparations as a project in itself, your time will run out. Even so, no matter how much time you allow, it will never be enough. You will still have a few late nights before you set off, but a preparation plan should help to reduce some of the stress. The key messages here are: *plan, start early and make lists of work.*

PROJECT MANAGEMENT

The task of getting the boat ready breaks down into three phases:

1 What equipment and skills will you need?
➤ Identify new equipment needed
➤ Do an electrical audit to make sure you have the power to match your needs
➤ Purchase equipment
➤ Identify any courses required

2 Getting yourself and the boat ready
➤ Fit the equipment
➤ Test new equipment
➤ Attend courses

3 Ready to leave
➤ Sea trials
➤ Do a shakedown cruise

➤ Pack the boat
➤ Victualling
➤ Leave your house secure

The timing of these phases depends on your circumstances, whether you are working and how much work or equipment is required. If you have equipment to buy, take the timing of the boat shows into consideration as they are good places to get discounts or just evaluate which equipment you want to buy.

From the boats surveyed, the average time taken to plan the trip was just over nine months, but this can be misleading as it really depends on how much of that time is devoted to planning and preparation. Our trip was planned over two years. We were both working; we wanted to fit various bits of equipment and take a sabbatical; I had to ask for the time off a year and half in advance. The last six months were dedicated to planning the trip around Britain, the rest of the time was used to ensure that we had the equipment we wanted for extended cruising.

A sunny spot in Salcombe

1 WHAT WILL YOU NEED?
New equipment for your boat
Identify well in advance any equipment that you require to be fitted.

Electrical audit
Prior to purchasing any electrical or electronic equipment, do an electrical audit to make sure that you have enough current to power your equipment. Identify the current (amps) required and the number of hours that you plan to run the equipment. Run two scenarios: at anchor and at sea and then calculate the total amp hour requirement for each scenario. Here is our audit:

DC device	Current draw (amps)	At sea		At anchor/harbour with no mains power	
		Hours used	Total amp hours = amps x hours used	Hours used	Total amp hours = amps x hours used
Refrigerator	6.0	3	18.0	6	
Radar transmitting	4.2	3	12.6		
Nav lights	0.5	8	2.0		
Instruments	0.6	16	9.6		
Instruments (night)	0.9	8	7.2		
Compass light	0.1	8	0.8		
Anchor light	0.3			10	3.0
Autopilot	2.0	20	40.0		
VHF	0.3	24	7.2		
Chart plotter	1.1	24	26.4		
Forward-looking echo sounder	0.95	1	0.95		
Sea-me active radar reflector	0.4	24	9.6		
Navtex	0.1	24	2.4	24	2.4
Heater	1.5	0		6	9.0
Chart table lights	0.4	1.5	0.6		

Saloon lights	1.4	0.5	0.7	3	4.8
Galley lights	1.4	1	1.4	1.5	3.3
Cabin	0.7	1	0.7	1	1.4
Radio	0.1			8	0.8
Mobile charging	0.6			2	1.2
PC charging	2.7			3	8.1
Contingency (10%)		14			7.0
Total daily requirement		**156**			**77.0**

Our total daily requirement ranged from a minimum of 77 amp hours up to a maximum of 156 amp hours.

If you have any AC equipment that you are planning to charge from a 12 volt system, then you can use an inverter. However, they are inefficient for converting DC to AC, as they lose 20 per cent during the process. So the amp-hours need to be multiplied by 1.2 to calculate the amount required. This should then be added to your total daily requirement. Here is an example of how you calculate your requirements:

AC devices	Power (watts)	Hours used	Total watt hours = watt x hours used
Microwave	600	0.5 (30mins)	300
Coffee maker	350	0.25 (15 mins)	88
Daily AC requirement			388

Daily requirement 388 divided by 12 volts = 32 amp hours x 1.2 = 38.4 amp hours

Only about 30 per cent of the battery capacity is usable, therefore to arrive at your required battery capacity, you need to multiply the total daily requirements by three. We needed 231 to 468 amp hours (Ah) (3 x 77 and 3 x 156) – but only had 240Ah available from our domestic batteries. Our engine is supported by a separate starting battery. There was just enough domestic battery capacity to cover our minimum requirement. So we upgraded the batteries to 320Ah (2 x 160Ah) – but we had to shop around to find batteries to give us the maximum amp hours and fit into the available space. We still had insufficient capacity. This meant that we had to run our engine during the day when the radar was on and/or use an alternative power source. We chose a wind generator.

You also need to ensure that you have the right alternator to charge your batteries. This is a complicated subject and I would suggest you refer to a specialist book.

Electrical independence

There are several strategies you can use to decrease your dependency on shore power:

➤ *Alternative power sources* Either wind, sun or a towed generator can be considered. Given the latitudes, only wind and towed generators are realistic for anything more than a trickle charge. We purposely went for a high output wind generator, Duogen D400 and we used to get 3.5 amps in 15 knots of wind. It also started turning at 6 knots, which is another important consideration, as well as noise.

➤ *Reduce power consumption* You can reduce your power consumption by the use of efficient appliances. For example, we fitted a Lopo LED tricolour navigation light with an all-round anchor light, which was excellent. It only draws 0.3 amps whilst at anchor, compared to 2 amps with our previous light, a saving of 17 amps for 10 hours overnight. This might not seem much, but if you consider that you need three times as much battery capacity, we would have needed an additional 51Ah of battery to use the conventional anchor light. If you do fit an LED light, do make sure it is compliant with the regulations.

➤ *Reduce the appliances that can only be charged by mains power* We used 12V chargers for both the PC and the mobile phone, as it is a more efficient way of charging than an inverter. That only left us only with the camera batteries that needed mains power.

➤ *Reducing battery charging time using a smart charger* A smart charger, such as an Adverc, does optimise your charging regime, which will reduce the time needed to fully charge your batteries.

➤ *Careful use of appliances* We used to turn on the heating whilst motoring into the harbour. This ensures that the heavy current draw, when getting the cabin up to temperature, is whilst the engine is on. Likewise, we would always turn the 'fridge on when motoring.

➤ *Carry a generator if your power demands are high* This is really only an option on larger boats. You may also wish to consider an intelligent energy system such as Victron, to make battery charging as efficient as possible.

Buying equipment

Here are a few tips for reducing the cost of buying equipment:

➤ Buy equipment in one go if you can; we prepared a long list of all electrical equipment and bought much from one supplier and received substantial discounts at a boat show. If you need additional cables or accessories, ask if they will throw them in free of charge.

➤ Ask for free delivery.

➤ Consider buying last year's models. With new equipment being launched at the boat shows, there are some real bargains to be had if you are happy to have an older model.

➤ Always ask for a discount – it doesn't cost you anything to ask!

Your own skills

It is not just the boat that you need to get ready. You need to look at your own skills. Some relevant courses might be:

➤ Additional RYA theory and practical navigation.
➤ Own boat tuition: most schools offer tuition on your boat.
➤ RYA Sea Survival Certificate: hopefully you will never have to use the skills learnt but this one-day course is also very useful if you are looking to update any safety equipment eg a liferaft.
➤ DSC VHF – if you have updated your VHF to DSC.
➤ Weather forecasting course: You may feel that your weather knowledge needs brushing up, prior to your trip. I can recommend Weather Consultancy Services Weather School run by Simon Keeling, who has an MSc in Meteorology and is a BBC TV Weather presenter. Whilst Simon is not a sailor, he has worked on many courses with Stokey Woodall, a very experienced and well-known sailor. More importantly Simon is a brilliant communicator who teaches weather theory with passion and makes it easier to understand. See www.weatherschool.co.uk or contact 01902 895252.
➤ RYA Diesel Maintenance Course: to ensure you can do basic maintenance and fault-finding.

2 GETTING YOURSELF AND THE BOAT READY

Fit the equipment

Leave plenty of time to get new equipment fitted. If you need contractors, they are particularly busy just before the season starts. Also, ensure that you leave enough time to test the equipment fully after fitting it.

Reducing the costs

If you do not have the skills to fit electrical and electronic equipment, you can substantially reduce the cost of installation, by running the cables through yourself. An electrician can advise you on the sizes of wires. If you are replacing any old equipment that is still serviceable, try selling it on eBay, we sold our old radar and antennae for £385.

Attend courses

Avoid doing this doing the month before you leave, as you will have many other things to do.

3 READY TO LEAVE

Sea trials

Prior to the trip, carry out sea trials, as it allows you to check that all the equipment is working and that you are up to scratch. Those that we carried out were:

- Putting up storm sails
- Putting up the cruising chute
- Putting in all three reefs
- Anchoring overnight
- Using dinghy and outboard
- Using emergency antenna
- Calibration of autopilot/radar
- Fire practice/use of fire extinguisher
- Familiarisation with flares
- Man overboard drill
- Using lifejacket hoods

Shakedown cruise

Once packed, a shakedown cruise will be a good way to check that you haven't forgotten anything.

Leaving your home

Don't under-estimate the tasks to be done when you are leaving your home for a couple of months.

Item	Task
House	Arrange for someone to check your house from time to time.
	Organise any additional house insurance.
	Arrange for someone to look after your front garden to prevent your house looking empty.
	Organise direct debits for any house bills that need to be paid whilst you are away.
	Set up a system for watering the garden or arrange for it to be done
	Empty freezer and refrigerator
	Reduce junk mail by using a mail preference service.
	Set up mail divert with Royal Mail.
Car	Arrange where to park or store your car.
	Check your road tax and MOT – you can register you car off the road at the end of your car tax period.
	Advise your insurers of what arrangements you have made.
General	Set up bank account access on the internet.
	Plan presents for birthdays whilst away.

5

STORES, EQUIPMENT AND KIT

Before our previous summer cruise, we made a list of everything we thought we should take, adding to it throughout the winter. Then when we packed the boat the winter before we left, we bought several large 'Really Useful' storage boxes and stored everything in them, ticking them off the list. This meant that loading the boat the following year was much easier as we knew where everything was and we knew what still needed to be purchased. The only things that we forgot to take were our thermals; we discovered this at 1:30am, just as we were setting off from Yarmouth, Isle of Wight.

Bear in mind that when you draw up your stores, equipment and kit list, it has to fit on your boat – weight is a consideration and you may need to make compromises.

GENERAL ITEMS TO TAKE
Clothes
You will be surprised how few clothes you really need. We took enough clothes to last us for three weeks and that was more than ample, as launderette facilities were regularly available. Once the weather improves, you can hang washing outside to reduce the cost of using a dryer in a launderette. A mini drying rack with clothes pegs attached helps to increase the amount you can dry in one go. Take a large zipped bag for laundry; it is amazing how quickly a washing mountain builds up.

Take a pair of waterproof trousers and a jacket for wearing ashore, as there is nothing worse than traipsing around ashore in wet oilies. Along with walking boots, they proved invaluable as they enabled us to make the most of our trips ashore.

Much of the time we were in oilies, even on sunny days. Here we are screaming along with only a scrap of jib out with 32 knots of wind, in the Sound of Sleat. As usual the waves look fairly flat; hence we took the picture to coincide with the waves breaking over the ketch

We followed the layer principle for sailing clothes: several thin layers are warmer than one thick layer. Breathable oilskins are a good investment, as you may end up living in your oilies and they will help to prevent dehydration.

Good quality boots which keep your feet warm make the world of difference. I lived in my Dubarry boots and at the beginning of the trip, they were fantastic. However, a word of warning about salt: after a while my feet got very cold at night, to the point they were so cold that they kept me awake during my off watch. I noticed that my boots appeared constantly wet, even if they had dried out in front of the heater vent. I realised that so much salt had been absorbed into the leather that when outside, even if it was dry, they would absorb water again. So when I wore the boots they would draw heat out of my feet as the water evaporated – hence my feet would get really cold. The cure was to soak my boots in warm water several times to get rid of the salt and then they kept my feet snug again.

Bikes

We used our folding bikes three times: a cracking ride along the River Camel in Padstow, and we cycled around Westray and along part of the Caledonian Canal. But in those places we could have hired bikes. If you are keen on cycling and do have room, make sure your bikes are compact and easy to access. Don't forget to take bike locks, puncture repair kit and pumps etc.

Galley equipment

On a short summer cruise you tend to eat out more as, after all, it is a holiday. But on a four-month cruise you are more likely to eat in quite a lot. So make sure you take the right equipment for normal cooking.

Barbeques

We enjoyed quite a few barbeques on board. We have a Cob BBQ, which you can place on the deck as the surround does not get hot. They are available from chandleries, though we bought ours cheaply on the internet. We were very impressed with the speed that it lit; only six charcoal briquettes were needed to cook a meal. Other BBQs that have been recommended are the charcoal BBQs that you can attach to your pushpit

SOME USEFUL BOAT EQUIPMENT

Heavy weather sails

For yachts, it is advisable to have a main that has three reefs and a set of storm sails. We carried a storm jib and trysail on board, both are orange for visibility, but thankfully we didn't need to use either.

Drogues

We carried a drogue, though mostly we were so close to land, it is arguable whether we would have had sufficient sea room to use it effectively. Though our primary aim was not to be caught out in such conditions.

Mast steps

It is essential to be able to be able to climb up the mast. For most, this will mean a bosun's chair and a lot of hard work on a winch. We were lucky that the previous owners had fitted mast steps. They are a real luxury and make getting aloft easy, and worth any reduction in performance.

Cockpit canopy

We didn't have a cockpit canopy and regretted it. It provides extra living space when it is raining and an area to hang wet oilies. A canopy also provides protection for instruments and from the elements when you are down below whilst still allowing ventilation from the hatch.

Autopilot

If you are single-handed or even a couple, an autopilot is actually an essential piece of safety equipment, as it allows you to navigate and undertake routines at sea. Even if you have a larger crew, I would say it is essential for your sanity. I love helming and would take the helm for a cracking sail but motoring can be tedious.

Heating

Having heating certainly made a difference for drying wet clothes and for keeping warm. It can be cold in late spring and we had ours on every night, up until the end of June.

Sometimes it is good to let the autopilot take over

Wetsuit and mask
A wetsuit with hood and a mask are essential equipment when dealing with fouled propellers (see Chaper 13).

FIRST AID AND MEDICINES
The general assumption on the cruise is that you can get medical assistance within twelve hours. Though it is not just first aid that needs consideration, you also need to look at non-prescription general medicines and any personal medication. We found that chemists were only available in towns. If you are taking prescription medicine take supplies with you; your doctor may give you a prescription that covers your requirements for the trip or you can arrange to have prescriptions faxed to a chemist en route. If you ever need to receive medical advice over the phone, then a list of medicines that you have on board will be very helpful.

We made up our own first aid kit and medicines box, designed to deal with the conditions below; a pharmacist is a good source of knowledge if you do the same. If you are taking any prescription medication, consult with your doctor as to the medicines that are safe for you to take. Sourcing first aid kits and medicines on the internet will reduce the cost considerably.

Category	Ailment	Items/comments
General first aid	Cuts	Plasters, micropore tape, zinc tape, wound closure (steri) strips, crêpe bandage, triangular bandage, fingerstall, first aid dressing (various sizes)
	Sprains	Tubigrip, Ice pack, Deep Heat
	Wounds	Savlon, TCP
	Fractures and sprains	Sam Splint, bandages
	Burns	Burnshield hydrogel and various-sized dressings containing hydrogel
	Eye care	Eye washes and eye bath, Optrex
General medicines	Colds	Beechams Day and Night tablets
	Sore throat	Betadine and throat lozenges
	Constipation	Senokot
	Diarrhoea	Immodium
	Insect bites and stings	Wasp Eaze, antihistamine and Anthisan creams
	Mouth care	Bonjela (mouth ulcer), Blistex (chapped lips) and Zovirax (cold sore).
	Pain	Ibuprofen, co-codamol, paracetamol and hot water bottle.
	Dehydration	Dioralyte
Preventative	Sunburn	Sunscreen is important even when it is cloudy as you can still get burnt. SF8, SF35, aftersun lotion
	Insect bites	An insect repellent is essential to combat the midges on the west coast of Scotland
	Seasickness	Stugeron, sea bands, Scopoderm patches and seasick bags
Equipment/general		Tweezers, thermometer, sterile scissors

MINIMISING AND MANAGING SPACE REQUIREMENTS

Weeks before leaving, you will make many trips to your boat with your car full to the gunwales and return with an empty one. You are then left with the challenge of being able to fit it all in and to be able to find it again. With limited storage facilities on board, you have to minimise and manage your space requirements.

Four rules for successful stowage

1 Reduce the need for storage space

- Start by completely emptying your boat to get rid of the stuff that you don't need; it is amazing how much junk you collect over the years.
- Use technology to replace some bulky items, such as replacing CDs with an IPod or MP3 player.

2 Organise your storage

- Improve accessibility for frequently used items.
- Try to stow items close to where they are needed.
- Plan the stowage of heavy items, so that they are balanced in the boat and stowed as low as possible.
- Group similar items together.
- Document where you have stowed things.
- Create more storage space by using the dead space more effectively.

3 Think about safety when planning

- Any fuels or flammable liquids should be stowed in a locker ventilated to the outside. On no account should they be stowed in lockers that vent to the bilge.
- Items should be stowed securely, so that they do not fly out and injure someone in a rough sea.
- If you have a fluxgate compass for your autopilot or radar, check that you don't store anything made of ferrous metal near by.

4 Protect your kit from the elements

- Ensure that any kit likely to be affected by moisture is stored in a waterproof container or bag.

Here are some ideas:

Reduce the need for storage space

Manuals Much of the space on our bookshelves was taken up by instruction manuals. One cruising couple scanned these into their computer – a task for next winter I think.

Music We eliminated the need for music CDs by wiring an iPod into our boat radio through a box available at car radio shops.

Organise your storage

Food lockers We had one food locker, where we kept items that we used regularly eg soups, pasta, food for lunch etc. In this locker, we stored food in manageable-sized containers; we bulk-stored the same items in other lockers in the bilge.

Baskets Lockers can easily turn into caverns where you can never find what you want without having to empty them. We used plastic baskets suspended on wooden rails; this allowed us to minimise the dead space.

Refrigerator We have a top-opening 'fridge, which used to be chaos, as everything you wanted was at the bottom. However, our 'fridge was transformed when we invested in some 'hamster' baskets, which are made to your measurements. These wire baskets stack on each other, enabling you to fit more into your 'fridge. It is also easier to get at items and it keeps your fridge cleaner, as food doesn't get squished or end up in a primeval swamp in the bottom. (www.hamsterbaskets.com).

Really Useful Boxes You need plenty of plastic boxes for general storage. We used the Really Useful brand to group things together. We chose several different sizes, and whilst not entirely waterproof, they keep moisture out. One was used to store all the pilot books when they were not needed, and this enabled us to place them low down in the boat. One held all the bike stuff, another had the dinghy and outboard bits: padlock, starting handle etc. Another one contained all the chargers that we had on the boat. We also used them for storing our clothes, as it prevented them from smelling of eau de boat.

Ship's papers These were all kept together in one folder.

First aid and medicines We separated these items into different boxes. Medicines that did not need immediate access were stored in the heads' locker. First aid was split into separate boxes: burns and eye washes, and general first aid. They were stored on a saloon shelf, and clearly marked so that we could grab the right box.

Tools The main tools were kept in a tool box but frequently used tools such as screw drivers (flat and cross-headed), an adjustable wrench and pliers, were kept in the companion way. This saved numerous journeys to unearth the tool box. If it is easier to access, you are more likely to carry out that quick two-minute job when it needs doing.

Emergency tools We have a set of bolt cutters and a gas-powered Shoot-it on top of the engine box, in case we needed to cut away rigging.

Spares We grouped spares together by type, trying to keep similar spares together. For small items like screws, fuses etc, we used fly fishing boxes to keep them separate. Those spares that we would need frequently or in an emergency were kept to hand, eg, engine emergency spares, such as an impeller.

Pilot books and charts We were lucky to have a long locker under the chart table for charts but most people store them under bunk cushions in large plastic wallets to stop them getting damp from condensation. We split the charts into legs in order of use. We highlighted the boundaries of all the charts that we had (including Imray) on the free Admiralty NP 109 publication. This was our reference guide to see which charts we had on board and it made it easy to see what number of chart was needed. It is also a good way of checking that you have all areas covered.

Day signals We stored the anchor ball and motoring cone in netting under the anchor locker lid. Each one had the appropriate length of strop and a carabine to attach it to the deck.

Where is it? book Each locker had a number and we noted down the location of everything in a little alphabetical index book. This is particularly useful if you have visitors onboard so they can find things easily themselves. But you do need to be disciplined to keep it up to date. For a while we thought we had a fatal flaw in the plan as we lost the book!

Even though we did all of this, we still needed to use two bunks (a quarter berth and forward bunk) as permanent storage, as the bikes took up quite a bit of space.

POWER CABLES AND OTHER ITEMS
Shore power
Most boats will need a regular dose of shore power. To ensure that you won't be left in the dark, take two shore power cables; in several places it was necessary to have a

very long lead. Also a splitter cable is very useful (ie it allows two cables to be plugged into the same power source) as this will ensure that you get power even when all the sockets are occupied. It is much cheaper to make one up from the various components. Or if you don't want to make them up, they are usually cheaper at a caravan shop. We also took a mains extension lead.

Batteries

Identify the sizes of all the smaller batteries you need on board and make sure you take spares of each type.

Bike equipment

We needed quite a few items for biking:

- Spare inner tubes and puncture repair kit.
- Helmets
- Pump, pesto adapter
- Panniers
- Bike locks

General items

Other useful items we took were:

- Wetsuit, boots, mask, fins, snorkel, gloves and waterproof torch
- Sewing kit: needles and thread
- Rucksacks
- Laundry bag and drying rack
- BBQ, charcoal and firelighters

BOOKS AND PUBLICATIONS

Pilot books will be covered in the navigation section.

Guide books

Much of your time will be spent exploring the mainland; you will find that many harbours in Scotland now have an award-winning heritage museum; but at £4–£5 a visit per person the cost soon adds up. We took the *Rough Guides to Scotland and Great Britain*; these were invaluable as we were able to learn about our new surroundings without paying a fortune. They were also helpful for choosing where to go, or where not to go.

Wildlife books

You will need some reference books to identify the flora and wildlife that you will see on your voyage (see Chapter 11).

A chance to explore new and unusual places – the Blinking Bridge, Newcastle

DOCUMENTS

The documents you need to take:

- Part 1 Ship's Papers or Small Ships Register Certificate (depending on which one you have).
- Passport – In case you go to France. Passports are not required for UK citizens visiting Ireland and vice-versa.
- Boat insurance documents.
- Driving licence (for hiring a car).
- Policy number and telephone number of home insurance company.
- VHF licence.
- Name, address and phone number of doctor and dentist.
- Two cheque books.
- National insurance number.

6

PROVISIONING

FOOD AND DRINK

Basic provisions are available in all but the most remote locations; there was always a village shop relatively close by. However, if you are at anchor on the west coasts of Ireland or Scotland, there may be no shop, or the nearest one may be a couple of miles away. Don't expect a wide range of products in these shops and you will probably pay high prices. Many bulky non-perishables items can be purchased prior to the trip and stored on the boat. This reduces the cost and the amount of shopping to carry without a car. This was also true for staple items like pasta, rice and cous cous, which can also bought in bulk and stored in 5-litre plastic jars.

In more populated areas there were shops within easy walking distance, though in some of the larger towns, a bus ride was needed to get to the big supermarkets. When moored in a town with a supermarket, we would check our route for the following week and if it included visiting remote areas, we would stock up with as much as we could carry. Rucksacks are really useful on these occasions.

Basic fresh produce was relatively easy to find. Though we did have the luxury of a 'fridge, and so were able to keep food fresh for longer. You also have the opportunity to taste local produce en route. We enjoyed Welsh lamb and mint sausages from local butchers, Grimbister cheese from the Orkneys, fresh scallops from several fishing villages and local fishermen sold us lobster cheaply in Whitby. See page 74 to find out what is a legal-sized lobster if you buy them direct from fishermen.

Wine boxes are ideal for a boat, though it is a good idea to keep a couple of bottles for social occasions on board other boats.

Quick meals

We always had a supply of quick meals on board, so when arriving in harbour late at night, instead of having to cook a meal from scratch, we could speedily heat up a meal. Ready-prepared pasta and sauces were our favourite standbys: a tasty quick solution for hungry sailors. Boil-in-the-bag rice was also popular.

Lunches

Tinned ham and corn beef were useful for sandwiches. Pitta bread makes a good alternative for bread in sandwiches as it lasts for a month. Fresh bread can be difficult to come by in certain areas, so you could try baking your own; the ready-made mixtures are very useful. Instant soups came in handy for lunches and night watches.

Fishing for supper

Many people on this cruise supplemented their food with the odd mackerel. Here are their tips for fishing on the move:

- *Cruise at about 3-4 knots.*
- *Use a paravane to keep the hooks below the surface; it takes the place of a lead on a trolling line. Unlike a lead they will not sink rapidly when cornering and will flip and bring the fish to the surface once hooked.*
- *Use mackerel feathers, preferably barbless hooks so when you bring up the line with all six hooks loaded with mackerel, you can keep the biggest and throw the rest back without injury.*
- *Don't let them die in the bucket. Rigor mortis sets in and they end up curved and you can't get them into the frying-pan.*
- *If you bait the hook with mackerel – you may catch bass.*

Lobster pot We caught several crabs in our collapsible lobster pot but, sadly, they were all too small and had to be set free. You need to bait the pot with fish and then place it near rocks but on a sandy bottom.

To be legal, lobsters should be more than 87mm from the eye socket to the back of the head section (carapace). Lobsters are being over-fished and in order to try to preserve stocks, fishermen cut V notches into the tails of female lobsters. These lobsters are not allowed to be eaten and must be returned to the sea to help increase the stocks. If you catch legal-sized crabs or lobsters, make sure you have a pan big enough to cook them.

GENERAL PROVISIONS

During the winter prior to your trip, it is worth recording your consumption of non-perishables. This allows you to calculate the quantities you will need for the entire trip. So you can buy in bulk, thus reducing your need to shop en route. Here are examples of the usage of some items used during the trip:

Item	Usage for two people
Kitchen towels	2 per week
Toilet rolls	1 per week
Washing up liquid	400ml per month
Shampoo	400ml per 6 weeks
Toothpaste	100ml tube per 2 months

FUEL

The availability of clean fuel is an important contributing factor to a successful circumnavigation:

Clean fuel

Prior to the trip, I had heard that there was likely to be problems with bad fuel; but of those surveyed, only one person came across this. Avoid a bad fill by taking the following action:

➤ Be selective about where you bunker up. Don't fill up from anywhere with a low turnover, especially at the beginning of the season, as there will be a higher chance of picking up dirty fuel, or fuel contaminated with water and the diesel bug.

➤ Change the fuel filter regularly, especially after a bumpy passage if you have had the engine running. Rough seas will stir up any sediment from the bottom of your tank. Fuel filters for our engine cost only £1.90 each, so we changed ours a minimum of every 100 hours if we had been motoring in smooth conditions and every 50 hours, if it had been a lumpy trip.

➤ Take a large clear jar, preferably one that can hold half a litre, as a fuel sample jar if you are considering filling up at a dubious refuelling point. The fuel should be left to stand for a short while and then you should check for suspended water or free water that will fall to the bottom.

Petrol

If your main engine runs on petrol, then you will need serious planning in advance as to where you can get petrol. Appendix 5 shows the availability of petrol at the quayside in 2007. In some places you may be able to arrange a delivery of petrol by tanker.

Also, petrol will be available in some roadside garages but you will need jerry cans to get it to your boat. However, in remote parts of Scotland and west coast of Ireland, it is likely to be long trip to find a garage with petrol. One couple reported having to hitch with four 20-litre jerry cans 60 miles there and back to get petrol in northern Scotland.

If you use petrol in your outboard, make sure you carry enough with you to last

Refuelling at Kirkwall. Photo: James Beattie

between stops. If your petrol outboard is your main engine, then seriously consider changing to a diesel outboard if you can get one to fit your boat. This was the advice of Sam Kent (*Silverwind*, Hunter Delta 25), whose biggest frustration of the trip was finding petrol.

Lead replacement gasoline (LPG)
LPG has replaced four-star fuel. As we have a treasured Seagull outboard, we needed LPG to run it. It is extremely difficult to find, so we carry it with us, plus we have a supply of an additive so that we can use unleaded petrol in an emergency.

Diesel
The availability of red diesel or green diesel (as it is known in Ireland) is good, but not available at every stop, so consult *Reeds Almanac*.

Managing your fuel
Regardless of the type of fuel you require, you need to ensure that you manage your fuel supply:

- ➤ In some places fuel is only available in jerry cans or drums. In Kirkwall, it was available in 25-litre drums but we had to borrow a hand pump to transfer the fuel on board.
- ➤ Plan your fuel stops. *Reeds Almanac* gives the availability of diesel en route, though some of this information was incorrect. So it is always worth phoning ahead and asking the harbour master if you are unsure of the availability. Also, check the opening times as some commercial refuelling points only open during the week. If you are planning to refuel by tanker, you will need to organise this several days in advance, as it is likely that they will only deliver to the port on certain days.

> Monitor your fuel consumption carefully by taking fuel level readings and log the engine hours run when you arrive at your destination. Knowing your hourly usage allows you to work out your motoring range and hence where you need to fill up.
> Always carry some spare fuel. We have fuel tank capacity of 200 litres but always carry 20 litres of fuel in a jerry can.
> If you use an additive, take enough with you for the trip.

Whilst private users of marine diesel will have to bear the increased cost as a result in the change in duty rate when used for propulsion, thankfully the use of red diesel is still permitted. Therefore there is no negative impact on the availability of diesel en route.

FUEL FOR COOKING
Gas
Butane gas (blue bottles) was readily available around the route and availability is marked in the *Reeds Almanac*, though you should always carry a spare. Note that in Ireland it is supplied by Kosan, a sister company of Calor Gas. They have a different connection and a different size, the smallest bottle is larger than the smallest Calor gas bottle used by many boats, but Calor gas bottles can be refilled in many larger towns.

Propane gas (red bottles) was more difficult to find; you may have to travel quite a distance to find it. One couple developed a little buggy that attached to their bikes to make it easier to transport.

Paraffin
Whilst it was available in many places, there is no information in the *Almanac*; therefore it is easier to carry your supplies with you.

WATER
Water is readily available for refilling your tanks; though you should work out how many days your water supply will last and monitor your usage. Our daily consumption was about 18 litres a day for two people, without a shower on board, so there was sufficient for 18 days. We filled up with water whenever the tank dropped below half full, or if we knew that we would not be in harbour for a while.

We were able to drink the water directly from the tanks, as a Penguin water filter was fitted, which removes any chemical tastes. It doesn't remove any bacteria, so you still need water purifying tablets, even if you are topping your water up regularly. Do take a hose and adapters, as they are needed in many places to get water from the taps. In many places, water can only be used for filling up water tanks so you are banned from washing your boats. This was mainly in the west coast of Scotland and in the Orkneys.

USEFUL EQUIPMENT

Equipment that you may wish to take onboard is shown below:

Water	Fuel	General
Hose pipe	Blow torch for paraffin cooker/gas regulator	Fishing line, hooks and paravane
Hose adaptor	Paraffin or Calor Gas	
Spray nozzle	Funnel	
Distilled water	Fuel additive	
Collapsible water container	Spare jerry can	
Water purifying tablets		
Water filter cartridges		

Sunrise over Longships, Land's End

7

MOORING AND ANCHORING

One of the pleasures of a circumnavigation is the wide variety of harbours and anchorages that you will visit on your cruise. This is particularly true if you are used to sailing in crowded waters, where marinas dominate and the opportunity to find a quiet anchorage is rare. On this cruise, you will experience everything from bustling fishing ports, where the harbour is still at the heart of the community, to deserted anchorages far from civilisation. The diversity of harbours does mean that you need to be prepared for different mooring situations. The survey showed that you need to be able to cope with anchoring, buoys, pontoons, marinas and walls, though most boats were able to avoid drying out unless they wanted to. The types of mooring used by the boats surveyed is as follows:

Mooring type	Yachts (31)		Motor boats (6)	
	Average number of days	Maximum number of days	Average number of days	Maximum number of days
Anchor	12	33	9	30
Buoys	10	31	10	21
Pontoon	11	32	9	37
Marina	34	76	25	37
Walls (afloat)	10	28	7	13
Drying	4	16	3	6

Each year, more and more marinas are being opened along the route. However, if your route planning is based on maximising the number of nights in a marina, then you will lose out on much of the real essence of a circumnavigation.

MOORING

Mooring buoys

There are two aspects to bear in mind when you are using a mooring buoy:

➤ *Be safe:* Make sure you pick a buoy that you know is regularly inspected and is rated for a greater tonnage than your vessel. Chafing of rope is a risk, so have the right equipment to minimise the chance of it being an issue: either moor with two ropes or have a section of chain spliced into your mooring buoy rope, or tie it directly onto the ring with a knot. Also watch out for chafing on the bow roller, so use strong material as a chafe guard, for example, plastic hose pipe or a section of an old fender. (See also page 83).

➤ *Be prepared:* Never rely on a visitor's buoy being available, so be prepared to anchor. Many buoys have no pick up, so threading a rope through the ring can prove tricky. We have a loop stitched in the end of our buoy mooring rope so we can pass it through the ring, and use the boat hook to pick up the loop.

The easiest way to pick up a buoy is to lasso it. Cleat off both ends of the long mooring warp, then coil the rope and split the coils so that you have half in one hand and half in the other. When you are nearly directly over the buoy, throw the coils up and out, so that the big loop goes over the buoy. This then enables allows you in slow time to make a more permanent attachment to the buoy.

There are still some buoys which are provided free of charge: the Orkneys and some

Tied up alongside Stonehaven quay

islands like Gigha. Bord Failte, Ireland's Department of the Marine and Coastal County Councils have laid a series of visitor moorings at selected locations. The moorings are large, coloured bright yellow and are labelled VISITOR – 15 Tons, though a small daily charge may be levied at some locations.

Walls

One of the challenges of walls is to have enough slack in your lines to cope with the range of tide, but enough tension to stay close to the wall as the tide rises. Weights such as an anchor angel, suspended on the mooring lines, are excellent for this. It is difficult to spring off a wall, especially at low tide. A boat hook is invaluable to push off, though make sure that you keep the hook part inboard and push off with the handle. In the worst case scenario, with the hook against the wall, it could snap or get stuck. We carried a 4ft (1.2m) wooden pole whose diameter was 3in (8cm), for this purpose; it stopped the boat hook getting damaged.

Fender board

If you value your GRP or wooden sides, then a fender board is a must. On many occasions you will need to use it when mooring against a wall, pilings or when refuelling. Many of the cheapest refuelling points are designed primarily for fishing boats that are a little more robust than a yacht.

They are easy to make, but the key is not to make them too heavy, as they become difficult to hold and manoeuvre. Ours is made from pre-treated timber, sanded to remove the rough edges. The dimensions are: 0.9in (2.2cm) thick, 5.4in (13.8cm) wide and 5ft 7in (1.6m) long. By drilling through the thickness of the board as shown in the photo, the board will hang horizontally and, more importantly, the side that faces away from the boat has no rope, ensuring that it will not get chafed through by rough walls. Two short lengths of 0.16in (4mm) cord are permanently attached to the fender board, making it really easy to tie it to the boat for storage along the gunwales.

If you have to moor against piles, it is very difficult to judge where the board needs to be located. Hang three fenders where the distance between each one is not less than the board; this enables you to move it relatively quickly to the right spot.

Mooring in canal locks

In canals, you will be required to moor against walls in the locks and at designated mooring spots: either a staging (fixed pontoon) or in a marina. Anchoring is also possible in the great Lochs that make up the Caledonian Canal.

As a canal has no tide, you do not need springs, just moor with a head and stern line.

The canals are always kept in immaculate condition; lock keepers maintain them with a real sense of pride: well tended gardens, paint work that is spotless. We chose an idyllic staging by Bellanoch Bridge on the Crinan Canal, a beautiful spot overlooking the River Add. The mooring posts were shiny black and we found out why – they had just been painted. The paint streaks on our lines now bring back happy memories of that night on the canal.

Entering the lock Make up both sides so that you can change sides quickly, as you never know what other boats in front of you are going to do. Tie a big bowline in the end of your lines and you can either throw it to the lock keeper or loop it onto an extendable boat hook, so that you can just pass it to the lock keeper. For this you will need two boat hooks on board. This makes getting the rope to the lock keeper much easier and was recommended to us by the lock staff on the Crinan Canal. It is far more successful than trying to throw the rope to the lock keeper. Make sure that you have long enough ropes, particularly in the sea locks. You may need to tie two ropes together.

Rising in a canal When in a lock, where the water will rise, it is important to keep the head rope tight, as the water will rush in at an alarming rate.

The water rushes in at quite a rate in a sea lock; this is Ardrishaig, Crinan Canal

Descending in a canal The water will be dropping so keep the stern rope tight. Though never cleat off any of the ropes, as you will end up suspended as the water disappears. If you have had to tie two ropes together, watch out for the knot so that it doesn't get stuck at the fairlead.

Fender cloth The locks walls are rough stone from which small flakes and grit can embed themselves into your fenders. A fender cloth will protect your topsides from this grit and you can clean off your fenders once you have left the canal. We only had one so always tried to tie up on the side that was protected by the fender cloth. Ideally have two fender cloths if you are planning to use a canal.

GENERAL MOORING EQUIPMENT

Warps

Ensure that you have enough warps for mooring in marinas, canals or alongside walls. In order to make it easy to identify the length of the warp quickly, use different coloured whippings to indicate the length.

Warp type	Comments
2 long shore lines	2 – 3 x boat length. These are needed for canals (especially sea locks), walls or rafting up. Remember that a wall requires 4 times the range of tide.
2 long warps	At least 1.2 x the length of the boat.
4 warps	At least 1 x the length of the boat.
Heavy set of warps	Needed for storm conditions.

Snubbers

Have four snubbers for the shore lines, so that they take the snatching strain rather than your fairleads or deck fittings.

Chafe guards

Chaffing can quickly slice through rope and warps, and has been a sailors' nightmare for centuries. Prevent it by the following:

➤ Use plastic hose or tough webbing covers that make a tube with velcro to prevent warps chaffing on the fairleads.
➤ If you moor next to a wall, use chafe guards to protect the rope at the shore end. A few hours rubbing against the stone will cut the rope like a wire cutter through cheese.

ANCHORING

If you need any more encouragement to anchor, then Holy Island should whet the appetite, where else would you use two castles as anchor bearings!

There are four essentials for successful anchoring:

1 Having the right equipment
2 Careful planning
3 Anchoring technique
4 Monitoring

Ground tackle

Good anchoring starts with having the right equipment. Each piece of your ground tackle: anchor, chain and shackle, should be sized correctly for the loads expected. You should also use seizing wire to secure the shackle key. Your anchor should at least be the recommended size for your boat but it is advisable to have an anchor one size larger than this. You should have enough equipment to be able to lay out two anchors if you are caught out in windy weather. There are many good articles in the boating magazines about anchors with the best holding power and everyone will have their own preference. You need to be able to hold in sand, mud, rock and weed. There will be some situations with rock or weed when only the fisherman anchor will hold. The minimum number of anchors you should carry is two; we took three anchors for a 38ft (8.5m) boat:

Type of Anchor	Weight	Comments
Spade	20kg	Bower anchor attached to 60m (197ft) chain. The convex shape of the spade anchor increases its holding power; we were extremely impressed with its performance, having replaced our old CQR.
Bruce	15kg	Spare 50m (164ft) chain not attached.
Fisherman	18kg	Taken in case we needed to anchor in weed. Stored below.

Type of rode/cable There are advantages and disadvantages of chain and line. With chain, you prevent chafing but the snatching is greater, plus the additional weight can be an issue up forward. The snatching can be reduced with the use of an anchor snubber. You can also have a mixture of both; chain with rope spliced onto the chain and this mitigates some of the disadvantages. The Clyde Cruising Club Sailing Directions recommend 60m (197ft) chain for anchoring in Scotland.

Anchor snubber An anchor snubber is generally a length of 33ft (10m) to 49ft (15m) nylon rope measuring ½in (12mm) in diameter, which is attached to the chain, either with a rolling hitch or anchor hook and made fast to a cleat or Sampson post. This will prevent any of the weight of the boat being held on the anchor windlass. It

Anchoring off Holy Island, with Bamburgh Castle on the sky line, and you can see the leading beacons clearly

will also act as a shock absorber, to reduce the effect of snatching on the anchor, which could cause it to drag. Hence you should use a rope that stretches easily, such as nylon. In normal conditions, we would let out 9–13ft (3–4m). It is important to attach the snubber to the chain, with a knot that can be released in a hurry.

Anchor windlass If you can fit an electric windlass on board, it has one big safety advantage over a manual windlass. You may have to raise your anchor a couple of times to get it to set correctly; it is less stressful therefore to use an electric windlass as you are more likely to set it correctly. However, this increases your power requirements.

Anchor chum or angel An anchor chum is a heavy weight that is attached to the anchor chain or rode and lowered down towards the anchor. There seems to be quite a varied opinion as to how effective they are. They are designed to reduce your swinging circle but it also has a dampening effect when the chain is snatching.

Riding sail Whilst the chances of gales are reduced in the summer, they can still occur. Tony Brimble (*Gitana* Crealock 34) rode out a force 9 at the end of May at anchor in Loch Ewe. If caught at anchor in a storm, a riding sail will help, as it reduces the amount and speed that the boat will yaw by reducing the swinging arc, as it keeps the boat's head closer to the wind. This reduces the snatching; which is what causes the anchor to drag. The very small sail is hanked onto the backstay and the tack attached with a strop to a strong point in the cockpit, hoisted on the mail halyard and the sheet led forward to a midship cleat. Whilst not essential, a riding sail will certainly help.

Bow fender We have a fender that protects the stem when we are anchoring or on a mooring buoy.

Anchor buoy and tripping line Make sure you mark 'anchor' on the buoy so that other boats don't mistake it for a mooring buoy. If you are anchoring near fish farms, it is advisable to set a trip buoy.

Careful preparation

When planning the location bear in mind:

➤ The prevailing wind direction and force, and the forecast wind direction and force.
➤ Direction of waves, swell and tide.
➤ Type of holding; depth and swinging circle.
➤ Local landscape – many anchorages, particularly in Scotland, may be well sheltered but subject to severe squalls in the lee of hills or in places where the wind may funnel down a glen.
➤ Other boats – though few anchorages that you visit will be crowded.
➤ Ease of exiting, if needing to leave at night.

Anchoring technique

Once in you have chosen your spot, you need to be open to changing your plan, depending on what you find – the echo sounder may reveal unforeseen obstacles. In many locations, the crystal clear water gives the opportunity to avoid weedy patches. You need to ensure that the anchor is dug in and set securely. Once the anchor is on the seabed, reverse slowly to allow the chain to be laid out straight, rather than dropping in a heap. Once four times the depth is laid out, secure the chain on a cleat or Sampson post and increase the revs to about 2000 and check that the boat is no longer moving. Then let out sufficient scope for the conditions; which is determined by the available space to swing, the current weather conditions (and those forecast), the depth, the tide or fetch, and the nature of the sea bed. Set your anchor snubber, take anchor bearings and then put the kettle on. In general we set 4:1 with all chain scope, but between force 4–6 we set 5:1 scope, force 7 and above, we lay everything we have, hopefully making up a 7:1 scope and possibly setting 2 anchors at about 45° in a fork moor, to cope with any forecasted wind change. If you have all-rope rode, you need to increase these by a factor of 2 (that is, force 4–6 will be 7:1, force 7 and above 9:1).

Communication

Good communication between the foredeck and cockpit is essential for effective anchoring technique. Have a commonly agreed anchoring procedure that you have practised, with standard key words or hand signals. This will become slicker the more you practise. We use the following for lowering the anchor:

➤ *Prepare to anchor* – untie/remove securing pin.
➤ *Stand by* – anchor to the water line.
➤ *Let go Xm* – controlled anchor drop, letting out Xm of chain – just enough to reach the bottom.

➤ *Xm down* – required chain now out.
➤ *Let go Ym* – slowly reverse and gradually pay out Ym of chain.
➤ *Ym down* – required chain now out.
➤ *Snub* – tie off anchor.
➤ *Anchor holding* – when reversing and the crew can see chain tension and lift.

For raising the anchor:

➤ *Xm* – said every time a 5m length comes over bow roller. Hand signals are also used to indicate the direction of the chain.
➤ *Anchor off* – anchor off the bottom.
➤ *Waterline* – anchor at waterline.
➤ *Stowed* – anchor secured.

If hand signals don't work for you, an alternative is to use walkie-talkies, as shouting is difficult in a wind. The best solution is to use voice-activated microphones which transmit when you talk.

If you are sailing single-handed, you need to set up a system so that you can anchor alone. If you have an electric windlass, you can fit remote controls in the cockpit. If you don't, you can take the anchor back to the stern (still with the rode from the bow roller) and drop it from the cockpit. This technique is covered in Roger Oliver's excellent article (*Practical Boat Owner* December 2003) about a single-handed trip around the UK published as a book: *Sailing Around the UK* by Adlard Coles Nautical.

Monitoring your situation

During the day you obviously need to take anchor bearings but at night you are unlikely to be able to see any lights in remote anchorages, so note your position on the GPS.

Anchor watch

You can set your GPS, chart plotter or radar to sound an alarm if your position changes by a defined amount. We used to set the GPS alarm to sound at 0.04nm (74m) at anchor. The next day we would forget that it was set and motor off, then wonder what the alarm was. Each time we were surprised at how far we had motored, before it sounded. It is a worthwhile exercise to test how long it takes before it sounds. It is more likely to wake you up just as you are about to the hit the rocks. Therefore, if it is very windy and you are expecting a wind shift, you should maintain an anchor watch. On a windy night, you are unlikely to be sleeping anyway!

DINGHY AND OUTBOARD

A dinghy is an essential bit of kit if you want to explore your surroundings when at anchor or tied up to a mooring buoy. An outboard is strongly recommended, as sometimes you will be quite a distance from the shore. Some landings for dinghies can be crowded and a long painter will allow you to keep your dinghy out of harm's way. We had a strop and padlock for the dinghy ashore but never felt the need to use it. The strop and padlock were, however, useful to secure our lifejackets in the dinghy to avoid having to carry them around. Though you won't need to do this everywhere – many remote communities don't lock their houses or cars.

If you have davits for a dinghy, you are very lucky, because blowing it up and deflating it is a real pain. Many people on the west coast of Scotland towed theirs, we tended not to, preferring to deflate it and tie it to the foredeck. If you chose to stow it, a 10-litre foot pump or a 12-volt electric pump takes some of the effort out of pumping it up each time. A LVM pump (costing approximately £70) takes less than a minute to inflate an average-sized dinghy. It uses about 25 amps at 12 volts; if you don't want to power it via crocodile clips and cables to the ship's battery, then it needs a special cable loop and plug. It is a good idea to wire an external deck plug direct to the domestic busbar via a 30-amp circuit breaker; it is sensitive to voltage, and anything more than 12 volts may cause it to burn out, so it comes with a warning not to use it when the alternator is charging.

We used a handy billy to raise and lower the outboard to the waterline. Ours is attached to a cage on the push pit, but I have also seen them on a single davit. It does make the task of lowering the outboard to the dinghy much easier. We also decided to carry a spare pair of oars, having once had an oar disintegrate. The list of recommended anchoring and mooring equipment we carried is listed below:

Anchoring and mooring	Alongside	Dinghy and outboard
Bower anchor and 60m chain	Fenders	Dinghy
Spare Bruce and fisherman anchors	2 fender cloths	Outboard
Anchor ball	2 boat hooks	Oars
Anchor chum	Heavy duty warps	Spare oars (not essential)
Anchor snubber	Warps	Fuel can
Anchor fender	Snubbers	Starter cord or key
Anchor light if not on mast head light	Chafe guards	Dinghy bag (for keeping things dry when in the dinghy)
Riding sail (not essential)		Small dingy anchor
50m spare chain and 50m rope rode		10-litre dinghy pump
Tripping line and buoy		Dinghy boarding ladder
Walkie-talkies		Fuel
Mooring buoy rope		

8

WEATHER

Normally we only really notice whether it is sunny or raining. During this trip we became far more aware of the weather: the cloud formations, their height, the wind strength and its effect on the water and the environment, as it had such a big impact on our everyday existence. It is unlikely that you are going to be at sea for days, unless your time available is very short. So you are always trying to work out: should I go today? What will the conditions be like? Will the harbour be sheltered? When is the next weather window? So you need to be able to:

➤ Check local weather conditions through local observation.
➤ Receive short to medium term forecasts (the next 6-48 hours).
➤ Obtain long term weather forecasts (3-7 days).

Local observation

It is important to check the weather conditions through observation; do your observations match the forecast? Though the site where you are moored is sheltered, the weather conditions may be totally different round the next headland. You can get additional information on local conditions through:

➤ *Local harbour master* For instance, in Newcastle, the marinas are several miles up the river but the harbour master will give you information about the conditions at the entrance. This is particularly useful for visibility, especially for your next destination.
➤ *Observation of surrounding features on land* In Inverness, the marina was sheltered from the wind but there was a tree on the opposite bank of the river. A

reading of force 2 in the marina could have misled us but when we saw the tree swaying vigorously, it confirmed a forecast of force 6 out to sea.

➤ *Observation of the clouds* A forecast of thundery showers whilst in Dartmouth might have seen us stay in harbour, but the lack of cumulonimbus clouds gave us the confidence to make the three-hour sail to Salcombe.

➤ *Observation of the barometer* It is invaluable and it will give you an indication of approaching bad weather.

However, you don't always get it right: when we left Helmsdale, it appeared relatively calm but we were in the shadow of the mountains of Sutherland and a few miles out to sea, we had 32 knots of apparent wind so we turned around and went back into Helmsdale. After all, we had four months to complete the trip!

Short to medium term forecasts

Receiving a short to medium term forecast will give you an indication of the weather for your current leg and, coupled with your local observations, will determine whether you should sail. It will also advise you of any changes in the weather once you have set off. With 48-hour visibility, you will have an indication as to whether you will be moving on the next day too.

Longer term weather forecasts

You need to be able to obtain and use, long term weather forecasts (3 to 7 days) to enable you to plan and pick your weather windows. You can do this either by interpretation of weather maps yourself or using someone else's forecast, and this will be determined by your skill level and equipment. Careful use of these forecasts will allow you to miss the really bad weather but gives you the opportunity to push on when there is a weather window. It enabled us to avoid some very nasty conditions, as our log entry for 16–17 May shows:

Weather to sail
16–17 May Dale to Holyhead

It was twilight when we raised the anchor. Neither of us had slept well, due to an uncomfortable swell that affected our anchorage off Dale, but we planned to be in Fishguard by about 1 pm. Out past St Anne's Head, the sun was rising but with little wind, we motored; cutting between the bird sanctuary islands of Grassholm and Skomer, we glimpsed comical puffins for the first time. We were unable to take the inside track past the islands but as it was calm, we cut in close to the Bishops and Clerks, some rocky outcrops with fast tidal streams that produce overfalls and whirlpools. Going through was quite dramatic – the sea appeared to boil but the tidal acceleration sped us quickly round St David's Head, then round to Stumble Head. We dropped the anchor just off Lower Fishguard. We needed some stores, so inflated the dinghy, went ashore and climbed into town (there is a reason it is called Lower Fishguard).

Back on board Mags got some sleep and I pottered and then got the long range forecast … ugh. Whilst we had been expecting strong SW winds on Wednesday/Thursday – the forecast had been upgraded to severe gale 9. Not fun in an anchorage. We had two options: ride out the storm at anchor then make for Holyhead after the storm had past with disturbed seas or head to a safer harbour straight away. My heart just wanted an early night and to be tucked up in bed, it had been a tiring day with an early start and not much sleep the previous night. But my head knew that the most sensible option was to run for Holyhead and make it in before the storm. We had a quick bite to eat, and then set sail. Ironically there was very little wind, and by 1am a thick fog descended. For the last hour of our trip to Holyhead, the wind started to blow and the heavens opened – an indication of what was to come. But safely tied up in harbour – albeit resembling drowned rats – we knew we had made the right decision. We listened to the howling wind and did not have to worry about whether the anchor was holding.

SOURCES OF WEATHER FORECASTS

In coastal waters around the UK and Ireland, you will have no shortage of weather forecasts. With the use of even the most basic technology, you no longer need to wake up at an ungodly hour to catch the shipping forecast. However, with so many sources of weather available and often conflicting ones, the danger becomes that you pick the forecast that you want to hear! So always make sure that the forecast bears a resemblance to what you are observing locally. If you do find that you have lots of conflicting forecasts, it is likely that the forecasters' confidence is low; hence you should be prepared for changeable weather.

UK Metrological (Met) Office

The UK Met Office provides extensive information, the majority of which is free. It covers UK and mainly Northern Irish waters and will provide one of your main sources of forecasts. Their free services are shown below and the equipment required to access them are shown in the table on page 93; note that all times are local:

➤ *Inshore forecast* This for 17 areas up to 12 miles offshore for the next 24 and 48 hours for UK and Northern Ireland. You will track your progress as you enter each new sea area which is bounded by a prominent headland. Some of the radio forecasts contain observations from 20 UK coastal stations.

➤ *Shipping forecast* Though provided for the offshore sea areas for the next 24 hours, these cover much larger sea areas and rarely include the variations that occur near land, so the inshore forecast is more helpful. Some forecasts contain reports from coastal stations, but as there are only 20 over the UK and Ireland, you will rarely be close to them.

➤ *Strong wind and gale warnings* A strong wind warning is issued for the yachtsman's gale: a force 6. One advantage of the inshore forecast over the shipping forecast is that winds over force 6 are monitored and strong wind warnings are issued.

➤ *Medium term forecast/three day forecast*

➤ *Latest marine observations* There are 36 marine observation points on the coast with hourly updated information. This contains some Irish coastal information. There are seven additional useful coastal waters observation points.

➤ *Surface pressure maps* These give eight pressure maps, for every 12 hours, for the next 84 hours.

The Met Office also have a chargeable service, MarineCall, which is accessed via phone (voice and text), online and fax, though most would not use fax from a boat. See website for details www.marinecall.co.uk or contact 0871 200 3985. Their forecasts are updated three times a day and are shown below and the equipment needed to access them is shown in the following table:

MARINECALL SERVICES AND EQUIPMENT REQUIRED TO RECEIVE THEM					
	Inshore	Coastal observations		Offshore	Weather maps
		Current	Next 6 hours		
Telephone	✓	Updated every 3 hours	Updated on an hourly basis	✓	
SMS (text)	✓	Forecasts are updated every hour at 30 mins past the hour and give data for the previous hour, the current hour and the next four hours. They are limited to a maximum of 160 characters. If you require more detail, use the phone service.		✓	
Internet	✓			✓	✓

➤ *Inshore 10-day weather* It starts with a 48-hour inshore waters forecast for your selected coastal area and up to 12 miles offshore, followed by a forecast for the day at 6-hour intervals and for the next 4 days. It gives wind direction, force,

Access via	Equipment required	Inshore forecast	Offshore forecast	Longer term forecast	Wind warning	Weather maps/ other
FW	Radio		0048 0520			
MW	Radio	Twice a day 0053 (9 areas) 0526 (17 areas)	0048 0520		Gale force winds at next programming break	
LW	Radio		0048 0520 1201 1754			
VHF	VHF Radio	Every 3 hours by Coast Guard for local sea areas updated 4 times a day	Twice a day for local areas		Every 2 hours for winds above F6 and above	
NAVTEX GMDSS	Dedicated NAVTEX equipment	Twice a day on 490HZ + actuals 4 times per day on certain stations	Twice a day on 518Hz	3 day forecast once a day on 518Hz twice a day on 490Hz		
	SSB receiver laptop					Weatherfax synoptic charts
INTERNET	Laptop and some mobile phones	All available on line updated twice a day			Strong wind warnings on receipt then repeated every 4 hours	Surface pressure with fronts are available on line and updated every 12 hours www.metoffice.gov.uk/weather /uk/surface_pressure.html Marine observations updated hourly

The types of forecast available free from the Met Office showing the equipment required to receive them. Check times as they do change periodically.

temperature, weather, visibility, sea state and pressure. There is also a national forecast for 6 to 10 days and an outlook for the month ahead. This forecast is often the one you see displayed by marinas and harbours.

➤ *Coastal observations* This covers current observations and forecasts from over 160 locations.

➤ *Offshore planning forecasts* 2–5 day planning offshore forecasts.

➤ *2–5 day surface pressure maps*

➤ *Talk to a forecaster* An expensive option at £17.00 flat rate, or £12 if you buy 50 forecasts (2007).

Met Eirean

Met Eireann provides forecasts for Ireland, including Northern Ireland, and covers:

➤ *Inshore weather forecasts* These are covered by two areas for Ireland for up to 30 miles offshore and are valid for 24 hours with a further forecast for the next 24 hours but for the whole area.

➤ *Hourly readings from 6 buoys (M1–M5) round the Irish coast located 10–60 miles offshore* There is one additional buoy M6, but this is some 200 miles to the southwest of the coast. There are also another five coastal observations.

➤ *Small craft warnings* These are issued if winds are forecast to be force 6 or above and are expected up to 10 nautical miles offshore.

➤ *Atlantic charts* These show surface pressure, rainfall, temperature and cloud for the current day at mid-day and 24 hours later.

Marine Weather Services

Location of Irish buoy network. Reproduction by kind permission of Met Eireann

Their free services and equipment required is shown in the table on the next page.

FREE SERVICES FROM MET EIREANN AND EQUIPMENT REQUIRED				
Access via	Equipment required	Coastal waters and Irish Sea	Wind warning	Weather maps
FW	Radio	0602, 1253, 1650, 2355 (evening times may vary at weekends due to sports coverage)		
VHF	VHF Radio	Every 3 hours by Coastguard every day	Gales warnings every 6 hours	
Internet	Computer/internet enabled phone	All available on line www.met.ie www.met.ie/forecasts/sea-area.asp		

NAVTEX

NAVTEX is transmitted over Global Maritime Distress and Safety System (GMDSS) and provides invaluable maritime information: the weather forecast, Subfacts (submarine information), Gunfacts (Gunnery range firing information) and other safety information such as navigational warnings. Though the ice reports are of less use!

They have regular broadcasts, and you can determine the information you receive by selecting the stations and type of information you require. The information is broadcast on two frequencies and you need both to receive both the inshore (490Hz) and offshore (518Hz) forecasts. The stations used are: Cullercoats (G), Niton (E, I and T) and Portpatrick (O). To receive actual weather reports, programme the message character V which is also called message character B2. If you enter Irish coastal areas, Valentia (W) and Malin Head (Q) will be used. Both inshore and offshore forecasts are available on NAVTEX. The easiest way to receive NAVTEX is via a dedicated receiver and it is extremely useful. Alternatively, you can receive NAVTEX through a SSB receiver and computer using specific software; the reception is improved due to the size of the SSB antenna. However, you need to remember to turn on your computer at the right time.

Access via internet

Apart from the UK and Irish Met offices, there are many other sources of weather forecasts. The internet provides a lot of free information; these are:

➤ *Wind Guru* was recommended by several harbour masters and also used by a couple of people surveyed. This site, primarily designed for windsurfers and kite surfers, is a free service which will give you a spot forecast around the coast.

Weatherdial

This is a chargeable phone service for weather reports covering the inland provinces, coastal waters and the Irish Sea. It can be obtained only from Ireland and is available by phone (but not SMS), internet and mail. Many harbours display the Weatherdial 5-day forecast, which provides invaluable swell information.

Reproduced by kind permission of MET Eireann

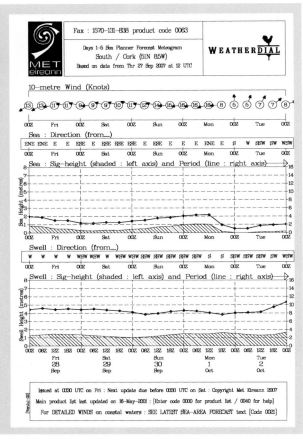

However, these are an output of model, which has a defined resolution (scale), and a spot forecast must therefore extrapolate the data beyond its accuracy. Also be aware that the models do not take into account any coastal effects. However, Wind Guru does acknowledge this and allow you to make wind modifications. The Wind Pro service which is available for a nominal fee does allow you access to more accurate models with improved resolution. More information at www.windguru.com.

➤ *Weather Web* This free site brings together lots of useful forecasts and charts from various sources in one place; it also includes satellite images. It provides forecasts, some of which are copies from the Met Office and others that are their own. www.weatherweb.net.

➤ *Real time data* Various sites show real time data. There is some limited data at the national buoy data centre which contains information from buoys and oil rigs around the coast www.ndbc.noaa.gov/maps/United_Kingdom.shtml. Another site is XC weather; this has more reports but the majority are land based. www.xcweather.co.uk.

➤ *Kevin Begley* has set up an extremely useful site with links to weather sites for Ireland www.begleys.com/weather.htm.

Forecasts requiring specialist software

A grib file is a compressed digital data file that enables weather data to be transmitted effectively across mobile networks (GSM, GPRS, and 3G), HF or satellite. When loaded into appropriate software, it can produce weather maps with coastlines and latitude and longitude grid lines; isobars are also constructed. Some software is free and others are chargeable and the differences are seen in the ease of data access, the presentation format, ease of use and data available. Many of the formats are very impressive but most come from the same model with little input from a forecaster. Therefore, they have their limitations when looking at coastal waters.

Charting software is also available, for example MaxSea, SeaPro, NobelTec and RayTech. Moving Data is a company that provides this service and software. It is easy to use because there is no requirement to obtain the data from email or a web browser; it displays the map of the area, the isobars, wind strength and rain. It then can show animated forecasts for the next five days. Fronts aren't shown but it does show sea state. Areas can be zoomed in on, but as the software is then interpolating the data, the accuracy of the forecast is not good. These global models are only accurate to about 100nm. Therefore, they should be used in conjunction with the inshore forecasts which are produced using models and human interpretation. www.movingweather.com

Weatherfax

Synoptic surface pressure charts showing isobars, fronts and pressure systems are available for up to five days ahead. Interpreting weatherfax requires a greater skill level as it is purely a synoptic chart, but it does give you an indication of the weather systems coming your way. They are transmitted from weatherfax stations at varying times of the day and the one used for the UK is the Royal Navy Fleet Weather and Oceanography Centre at Northwood.

Dedicated weatherfax hardware is available or it can be received using a single sideband receiver (SSB), PC and some software, for example: Mscan Meteo or JVcomm. Free software is available but it doesn't provide automatic tuning and interference can be a problem. We used Mscan Meteo and had no problem with either. You just need to remember to turn it on at the right time to pick up the broadcast. With this software you can also access NAVTEX and Radio Teletype (RTTY). RTTY is of limited use as it only covers the North Sea and English Channel. Some manufacturers are now making receivers that allow synoptic weatherfax charts to be shown on electronic displays.

Harbours and local information

Most harbours will display a local forecast for the area. Orkney Harbour radio gives an excellent weather forecast (and navigational warnings) twice daily. They give the forecast for three six-hour blocks, followed by a forecast for the next 12 hours; the day after will be a general view.

Talk to a weather forecaster

If you have very conflicting forecasts or you need help with understanding the long range forecast, it can be helpful to talk to a weather forecaster. We used Simon Keeling's Weather Consultancy (0906 515 0046). It costs £1.5 per minute (2008), with a call lasting 2–3 minutes which is charged to your mobile phone; this is cheaper than the Met Office. From Ireland (00441902 895252), there is a flat fee of £15 (2008). If you do get a forecast from a weather forecaster, make sure you ask them what is the confidence level of their forecast. If it is very difficult to predict, their confidence level will be low, so expect changes.

Survey results for forecasting

Those sailors I surveyed used a combination of methods to access forecasts; on average using between two to three different methods. All access methods have their advantages and disadvantages: VHF reception can be poor in some lochs in the north-west of Scotland but we found that we did get mobile reception so were able to either access the internet or phone the Coastguard when in port.

NAVTEX reception from the Portpatrick station, using dedicated NAVTEX equipment, was poor above the Crinan Canal and for much of the west coast of Scotland. This was a common experience, although it was better with SSB but you had the disadvantage that you needed to remember to turn it on at the appropriate time, plus you have the additional equipment cost. Even so NAVTEX, along with forecasts from Coastguard, BBC radio and harbour masters made up the primary source for forecasts.

Text 2%
Met Office weather maps 4%
Internet 10%
Harbour masters 13%
Forecaster 3%
Weatherfax 3%
Mobile phone 2%
BBC radio 16%
Coastguard 24%
NAVTEX 19%

COASTAL CRUISING

The real challenge for any forecast is that the winds close to the coast are influenced by the shape of the land, the differential of land and sea temperatures, the different frictional forces over land and sea and the state of the tide. As the majority of your cruise is spent in coastal waters, you will encounter many of these effects:

Seabreezes

Seabreezes are caused by the imbalance in heating between the land and the sea, when the land heats faster than the sea. A seabreeze usually starts to develop on cloudless summer mornings. As the land heats up, the air above it rises. To replace this rising air, cooler air is drawn in from the sea and an on-shore breeze develops, known as a 'seabreeze'. On a hot summer's day, a typical seabreeze can extend about 15 miles out to sea and may add 10 knots to the overall speed of the wind. The seabreeze tends to reach its peak in the late afternoon and early evening before dying away at dusk as the land loses its heat. Accompanying the seabreeze may be a line of cumulus cloud along the coastline, on what would otherwise be a cloudless day.

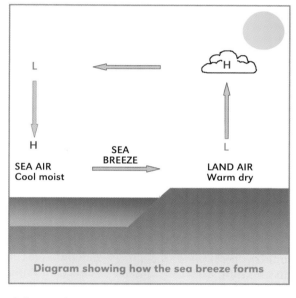

Diagram showing how the sea breeze forms

Seabreezes don't always form. On of the reasons for this may be that the wind is blowing off-shore and the on-shore sea breeze needs to overcome this competing flow. There are days when this effect simply delays the onset of the breeze, but other days where it can disrupt it altogether.

Initially the seabreeze will be blowing directly on-shore, but during the day the winds gradually veer; eventually blowing parallel to the shore. If you are on a clockwise circuit, this can be very frustrating as you have head winds on many afternoons along the North Sea. I know this from bitter experience.

Headlands, bays and islands complicate the picture when predicting the direction and strength of the seabreeze. A headland will strengthen a seabreeze; a peninsula will see the wind blowing towards the main land mass and this can lead to a build up of air over the land mass, perhaps triggering showers or thunderstorms. A bay, however, will see a weakening of a seabreeze.

Land or offshore breeze

The land, whilst it heats up faster than the sea, it also cools down faster. Given certain conditions, such as a clear sky at night, calm conditions and sea temperatures at their maximum, as in autumn, then the sea can be warmer than the land. You then have the reverse situation to a sea breeze. An off-shore breeze can establish itself in the early hours, when the air from the land fills the space of the air that is rising over the sea. It can be felt up to 10 miles out to sea; it reaches its peak at 3am and dies away at dawn.

Katabatic winds

Katabatic comes from the Greek *katabaino* – to go down. This word is used to describe exactly those winds that go down – from mountains to the area below. In Scotland and Wales, on clear nights in the high mountains and hills, the land loses heat quickly, a large pool of cold dense air builds up and is trapped until it eventually spills over the side of the mountain, and rushes down the glens and valleys producing katabatic winds. They can be strengthened by the shape of the surrounding landscape. It can catch you out at anchor, when the wind can increase by two levels on the Beaufort Scale and then return to a gentle breeze later on.

The effect of the landscape

As a river changes direction and speed when in contact with rocks and banks, so does the wind round headlands and valleys. A gentle breeze can bend more than 90° round a headland. A slightly stronger breeze may bend slightly less, around 25°. A force 7 wind will only change direction marginally around a headland. However, it also accelerates around headlands sometimes by up to 30 per cent. Islands will also disrupt the wind, so be ready for changes in direction and strength.

Land exerts more drag on the wind than the sea and so when the wind blows parallel to the coast, it causes changes in direction. Winds will converge or diverge depending on which side of the wind the land is. If there is an east wind on the south coast of England, or a west wind on the north coast of Scotland, then they will converge with the shoreline (up to about 20 to 30°). This results in a stronger band of wind within about three miles of the coast – an increase of wind strength by up to 10 knots – and it veers towards the coast. When winds are blowing in the opposite direction, they diverge which may result in lighter winds near the coast, unless affected by land and sea breezes. When the wind blows at right angles to the shore, there is little convergence or divergence. However, an offshore wind does veer by 15° over the sea.

Sea fog

Sea, or advection, fog is a real hazard. Fog forms when the warm air is cooled from below, until it can no longer 'hold' the moisture that was previously contained within, so some of this vapour condenses. When the air cools to its dew point, the moisture held in it condenses into very small droplets. The dew point indicates the amount of moisture in the air. The higher the dew point, the higher the moisture content of the air at a given temperature.

Dew point height	Fog type
Dew point of air above the sea is very high and generally the sea temperature is lower.	Extensive or widespread fog
Dew point of the air a little above sea temperature and in some places not above it.	Fog banks
Dew point of air is only just above sea temperatures in some patches.	Fog patches

The conditions for fog can occur when moist warm air passes over cold water and so usually occurs between April and September. It is important to note that sea fog can occur at any time of day accompanied by quite strong winds. With winds above force 4-5, the result may be low cloud and poor visibility rather than fog.

Fog drifting in from the sea up the River Dart

North Sea haar On the east coast of Scotland, sea fog is known locally as a haar or North Sea haar, and no doubt you will come across it. It is most likely to occur on the east coast, or over the Northern Isles during early summer, before the notoriously cold North Sea has started to warm up. With an easterly or south-easterly wind, a haar is possible as the warm air from the Continent passes over the middle of the North Sea (where temperatures are warmer) and so the air becomes warm and moist. It then arrives at the east coast of Scotland where the temperatures are colder. The east coast of England is also affected but here it tends to be known as a sea fret.

North Sea haar taken by NERC Satellite Station. Photo courtesy of the University of Dundee

South coast A warm moist south-westerly wind from the Atlantic in late spring and early to mid summer can result in sea fog before the inshore water temperatures have increased.

When will it disperse? Inland, the fog is likely to disperse as the land is warm. So if you are stuck in a harbour, it is worth venturing inland for a day's exploring and you are likely to find a glorious sunny day. Also the fog is likely to disperse if you can go up river or into a pool of trapped water, as the water temperature is warmer. Sunshine is needed to burn off the fog; it warms the air and allows the condensed water to be turned back into vapour. However, if the fog is very thick, the sun is unlikely to burn through it.

9

STAYING IN TOUCH

You will be surprised at how many people will be interested in hearing about and following the progress of your trip: family, friends and even total strangers. To allow you to share the progress of your cruise with the maximum audience, take advantage of some of the technology available, though the disadvantage is you will fill your boat up with the various chargers!

MOBILE PHONE

Much of your time will be spent at the edge of a network operator's coverage, so check on their websties to see if it covers your intended track. In 2006, only Vodafone had total coverage of the UK coast and there were only two places on our route, where we didn't have coverage in harbours and anchorages: Holyhead and Eyemouth, though the latter was only at low tide. However, most of our harbours and anchorages were on the mainland. If you are visiting the islands and very remote anchorages, you will find areas where there is no reception. If you ask the locals, they will tell you the exact spot on the island, where you can get coverage.

Some phones have the ability to connect to the internet via the wireless hotspots network (WiFi). Therefore, you can access the internet without going through your network provider and use downloadable software called Skype to make free calls. However, this service will only be available close to large towns and certain marinas where WiFi hotspots are available.

If you are making international calls from Ireland, make sure you use the right network provider, to reduce your roaming charges. Your own network provider will advise you which one you should use.

WEBSITE

We created our own website (www.ituna.info), so that we could publish our log on a daily basis. It was free and enabled friends and family to follow our progress – better than sending postcards! It proved very popular and our friends and family really appreciated it. We had about 775 different people following us in July, with an average of 250 hits a day. Several crews found it a chore to write up their log regularly, but once you have returned, it is a great record of the trip.

The success of your website will depend on your skill level. Our site contained:

➤ A chart showing our current location and our daily track.
➤ Photos.
➤ Daily log – the front page had the latest log entry and a recent photo.
➤ Boat statistics.
➤ Itinerary ie, where we were planning to go. This is useful if anyone is planning to meet up with you.
➤ Contact details. Email and phone only, don't put your home address on the site, as you will be advertising the fact that you are not there. If you are concerned about getting lots more spam mail, as a result of displaying your email address, you can put a clue about it, for example, 'replace X by J in XSmith@aol.com.'
➤ The facility to count the number of hits.

In Appendix 6 there is a list of some useful websites that were available at the time of writing. However, it is impossible to know how long they will remain available.

Basic web knowledge

If your knowledge of building a website is basic then use a weblog or 'blog'. Blog sites have special software which allows you to upload information to your website at the click of a button. Some even allow you to upload pictures and text from your phone. A blog also allows others to post comments easily. With a blog you will have less control over the format of your site, but it is easier to create and update if you do not have specialist knowledge. There are two types of suitable blog providers:

➤ *General service providers* These allow you to create a blog and upload photos and text from computers, and in some cases, from phones. Some are free and others charge; www.blogger.com which is owned by Google is free. Other examples are Yahoo 360 (http://360.yahoo.com), MySpace (www.myspace.com). A blog can be accessed by anyone who finds it but the content that you update is password-protected.
➤ *Specialist provider* A service provider which caters specifically for the marine market eg, www.Yachtplot.com. The advantage is that you get location and track information as part of the package. It is a closed blog and can only be accessed by people who have the password. You can use the internet to update your site, as well as other methods such as: SSB, fax, Iridium phone, though these methods are

unlikely to be of benefit to those cruising around the UK. There is a cost for this service which is determined by the length of time you wish to have your site hosted.

Intermediate knowledge

You can create your own website, which gives you the freedom to format your site as you wish. This is done by creating html templates, which you can update online and are created using a programme such as MS Front Page. If you are experienced with knowledge of html syntax and a text editor, then you can achieve the same result. This has the advantage that you can prepare the format and layout in advance, and then cut and paste the content. If you want some flashy features, then you will need java script knowledge. There are several ways to get your website hosted:

➤ *Most internet service providers provide web space* Some will offer limited free space with your subscription but for most you will pay according to the space required. The disadvantage is that you can't choose your URL (web domain name).

➤ *Some hosting is free in return for advertising space* Again you can't choose your own URL and you need to check the advertising requirements. Some can be discrete banners but others have heavy advertising demands.

➤ *Web hosting companies* The advantage with these is that you can choose your own domain name. These companies charge for their services, though it is possible to get free space. New web hosting companies that are trying to establish themselves often have offers of free web space. You can find out about such offers from the magazine .net (www.netmag.co.uk), this is also a good place to search for domain name providers. Equally enter 'free web space' into Google and you will get many sites. We used 1 and 1, which allowed us a free hosted site for three years.

Some providers have useful standard functionality, such as photo albums, to enhance your site. Once your website is created, always keep a copy of your full site on your laptop as a back up.

You need to consider how you will update your website. With some providers, you update each file individually, which can be tedious. Those that provide an FTP server solution are the best, as this allows you to use the drag and drop functionality similar to Windows Explorer, so it is much easier to use.

If you want others to find your website through search engines such as Google and Yahoo, then you will need to register your site with them. More information on how to do this can be found on their pages.

Creating an interesting site

Here are a few tips on creating an interesting website or blog:

➤ Many of your readers will not be boatie types, so don't exclude them by using nautical language, or if you do, explain what you mean.

➤ Make it interesting to read, describing places and the voyage, rather than a synopsis of courses and buoys passed.

➤ Keep your website updated frequently; if it stays static too long, people will either worry or lose interest in following you.

➤ Don't make it too flashy; it can take too long to load and can be a real turn off.

➤ When mailing your friends with the link to your site, make sure you check that the link in the mail works – before you press the send button.

➤ Include a map, as most people will have no clue as to the location of many of the places you are visting or the headlands you pass. You need to be careful about copyright and should obtain permission to use a copyrighted map. You can show your actual position displayed on a chart, using equipment hired at approx £5 per day from providers such as MarineTrack. Or if you have a GPS enabled Nokia phone, you can do this free of charge using sportstracker (www.sportstracker. nokia.com).

➤ Try to communicate your emotional highs and lows – people find this fascinating.

Making decisions
26–27 May – Kirkcudbright to Campbeltown

The engineer had real problems in removing the seized bolt from the alternator; he eventually drilled it out in his workshop. By the time it was fixed, we had missed the morning tide. A blow was expected on Monday, so if we wanted to get to Campbeltown before the windy weather, we needed to leave sooner rather than later. But that meant the evening tide, which was after dark. It had been interesting coming in through the windy river in the daylight, in a flat calm, so a night exit would be very tricky and it was already windy: F5 gusting 6. We went for a walk round the town to contemplate our decision: to stay until after the windy weather or head out on the night tide.

Kirkcudbright is an attractive town; brightly coloured houses line the streets and in the centre is an old 16th century fortified house. In almost every street there is a gallery. It is also known as the Artists' Town through its connection to the 'Glasgow Boys', a group of 19th century Impressionist painters.

We decided to 'go for it'. As it is tidal, we couldn't leave until 10:15pm. So we had to sit around waiting. We always felt apprehensive prior to a big passage; in this instance the prospect of navigating out of Kirkcudbright at night, then sailing round the Mull of Galloway, which has a fearsome reputation. It is the anticipation which is worse – why were we leaving a nice secure berth and venturing out on a windy night?

We eventually set off, counting the flashing buoys as we passed them; all went well until the light on the depth sounder stopped working. A depth sounder is essential on this shallow river. Mags grabbed a torch and, apart from two buoys that weren't lit, which gave us a heart-stopping moment, as we narrowly missed one, we made it out safely. In the bay, we had 27 knots of wind so we needed three reefs in the mailsail; we settled the boat on course and Mags went off watch. We were sailing into the wind (typical), the tide changed and was now with us. However, the wind was now in the opposite direction to the tide, and raised quite a sea, with sharp steep waves which knocked the boat back. By now we should have been well on our way to the Mull, but our progress was painfully slow. It became obvious that we wouldn't make it past the Mull before the tide changed. With spring tide against us, we would be lucky not to go backwards. I started to question my decision to leave Kirkcudbright. I considered the options: we could go back to Kirkcudbright – but we would have to get back in time for the next high tide; go to Douglas on the Isle of Man – but that meant going back; or soldier on and accept that for the next six hours we would be looking at the same view of the Mull. We decided on the latter, I headed off watch and three hours later when I got up, the view was still the same. But with the tide with the wind, the sea had calmed down considerably, so I cut inside close to the Mull to pick up a back eddy and we started going forward at last. But when we turned right to go up the North Channel – so did the wind, so we were sailing into it again.

The next weather forecast was showing N5–7. We would be heading north, bang into the wind, so again we would make little progress. Portpatrick, a small fishing village, was an option, but on a falling tide and with a strong onshore wind, it was not a sensible one. Thankfully, we made good progress up the North Channel with the tide and when we got to the top of the Mull, the northerly wind had not yet set in so, we decided to make for Campbeltown. We still had three reefs and at 30 knots of wind, we were steaming along despite the tide being against us. We passed the Ailsa Craig (Paddy's milestone) a distinctive lump of rock, Mags was back in familiar waters and before long it is 'Land Ahoy' as we spotted the Mull of Kintyre. Mags did a kind of rendition of 'Campbeltown Loch, I wish you were whisky, for I would drink you dry'. It was not long before we picked up the light on Daavar Island, which guards the seaward end of the loch. By the time we passed the island, it was dark, which was a shame, as we would have sailed right past Mags' parents' house. By 2am, some 30 hours later, we were tied up safe and sound. Getting there gave us a huge sense of achievement, we had seen some awesome scenery and we had a great sail ... that's why we do it.

INTERNET CONNECTION

There are several ways of connecting your computer to the internet from your boat:

➤ *Using your mobile phone as a modem* A phone needs no additional kit other than a means of connecting it to your computer, usually via a cable. The speed you achieve depends on which service you have subscribed to and your location. Most operators provide GPRS (57kps) as normal service. You can subscribe to a 3G service (384kps), but you need a phone capable of making 3G calls. However, availability of the 3G service is currently limited to major towns and cities. The bigger the kps, the faster the data is transmitted.

➤ *Data card which fit into the network slot on your computer* The data card contains a SIM card, similar to the one used in a phone. You can buy the card separately and then use it with your SIM card from your phone but you will only achieve the speed of the service you have purchased. You can also buy the data card with its own SIM card and then you buy data by mega bytes. Usually there is a fixed price for a certain amount of data and then a variable price after that. You will access a network using 3G or GPRS depending on your location.

We used a Vodafone 3G card and a package of 25MB for £25 per month (2006). This gave us 25MB of GPRS and 25MB of 3G. However, most of our 3G allocation went unused. We chose Vodafone because, in 2006, it alone provided network coverage over the whole coastline. Through the internet we were able to manage our finances; it still seems amazing to be able to manage your bank account whilst at anchor.

Banking in Tobermory

➤ *Wireless network (WiFi)* This is the fastest connection to the internet available from a boat. You connect via hotspots, which are available in some marinas. Its speed depends on the hotspot that you are connecting to, but usually provides similar speeds to broadband. To use it, you need a WiFi enabled PC, though sometimes you may need an external device such as a SmartBridge ethernet adaptor to get connected in a marina. The hotspots are provided in some marinas by Square Mile (www.squaremileinternational.com).

➤ *Internet cafés* If you don't have a laptop, you can still gain access to the internet through the use of internet cafés. However, you can't always predict where you will find them.

LAPTOP

We needed to buy a laptop for the trip and one of our selection criteria was battery life, we chose the model using information from the magazine *What Laptop*. You can buy a ruggedised laptop, also called a 'tough book', but given that the price is approximately four times the price of a standard laptop, it is cheaper to replace a standard one a couple of times before a tough book makes financial sense. Here are some tips for getting the best out of a laptop:

➤ The battery life can be extended by disabling the wireless card and reducing the brightness of the screen when running on battery. This can usually be set up as a default in the power options when running on battery power.
➤ To maintain the battery in top condition, never leave the laptop charging once the battery is full.
➤ Make sure that you store it in a safe place: a padded bag is ideal.
➤ If you are using the laptop to run navigation software then make sure that it is securely fixed to the boat.

PRINTER

Not all our friends and family could access the internet, so we printed off a log every couple of weeks – both the text and some photos. Miniature A4 colour printers are produced by several manufacturers for just under £200. These 'snail mail' versions of our log were very much appreciated.

EMAIL

There are two ways to receive emails whilst away:

➤ You can log onto your email account with a computer, either from your boat or an internet café.
➤ Via Push Mail, where your email is sent to your phone, for example by using Nokia Communicator or a Blackberry. This is set up via your network operator and has the advantage of not needing a laptop to get access to your mail. Also you are aware of mail as soon as it arrives, assuming you have network coverage, though it can be argued whether this is an advantage or not!

Working offline

We used our home AOL account over the internet via the laptop but now realise this was a mistake, as it doesn't give you the ability to work offline. Therefore, every time you read an email, it has to be opened from the server, adding additional communication costs. So make sure your email service provider allows you to use email software to enable you to work offline. You will need a POP3 account to be able to work offline. Your email provider should give you this information so you can configure email client with your POP3 email server. In MS Outlook, it is an option in tools>email account>add new email account>choose POP3, and then you add the server name.

PHOTOGRAPHY

A camera is a mandatory piece of equipment for this cruise; whether using a film or digital camera, you have to be able to capture the moment.

Digital cameras

A digital camera is essential for updating your website/blog. The other advantage is that you can take hundreds of photos; so you are more likely to get that picture in a million. The disadvantage of using a compact digital camera is the delay between pushing the button and the picture being taken. This is frustrating, especially if you are trying to photograph dolphins. We have lots of pictures of empty sea – where once they had been. Some tips for getting the best from your camera:

- Use a large memory card to prevent it from filling up at the wrong moment. We had a 1 GB memory card, to cope with the number of photos.
- Keep your camera within easy reach. Use a waterproof box in the cockpit locker, this way you will have your camera to hand for taking photos.
- Use a camera with a high number of pixels, as it determines the picture quality. A higher number of pixels is required if you intend to enlarge your photos. The photos in this book are taken with a 5 mega pixel camera.
- Use a camera with a wide-angle lens. It is a real challenge to capture the scenery and the boat. A wide lens of 12 or 18mm will make a huge difference. Even some compact digital cameras have a wide-angle setting. However, it is invariably difficult to do some of the landscapes justice, even with a wider lens.
- When sending the pictures in emails, make sure you save them separately as best compression ready for mailing; this is available in Options when saving it. This will reduce your communication costs.
- Carry a spare camera battery.
- Save pictures as TIFF files if your camera allows this. Every time you open a photo which has been saved as a JPEG file, it loses a small amount of detail, as the data is compressed. A TIFF file doesn't compress the photo, hence it doesn't lose any quality.
- Do take an editing software package, this can dramatically enhance your photos just by careful cropping and so improve the look of your website.
- A polarising filter will really help to capture the colour of the turquoise water.

If you are using a 35mm film camera, remember to take spare batteries and plenty of film.

Video cameras

There are some scenes that a still camera can't capture adequately. We took a video camera but rarely used it; this was probably because it was the first time that we had used one. I now realise that it would have given us the ability to capture the dolphins and the sheer scale of the beauty of the coastlines, the west coast of Scotland in particular.

MAIL

We set up a redirection service for our mail for four months at a cost of £48. Our mail was redirected to my mother, who would sort out what needed to be forwarded and what could wait until we got back. If we knew we were going to be in a harbour for a while, we would ask her to send the mail to the harbour master of the next planned port. That way we never had to hang around waiting for the mail to arrive. She marked the mail with the name of the boat and 'please keep for visitor'. Also we would phone up the harbour master in advance to check if it was permissible to send mail. Most mail arrived the next day, but be warned that in the Highlands and Islands you need to allow an extra day for it to arrive. Before starting your cruise, try to cut down the amount of mail that needs to be sent on to you:

➤ Avoid junk mail by using the mail preferences services www.mpsonline.org.uk or MPS Registration line - 0845 703 4599.
➤ Set up bill payments including visa cards by direct debit.
➤ Set up internet banking so that statements can be obtained over the internet.

BUSINESS CARD

One of the joys of cruising is meeting new people and so you are always exchanging details. We created a business card with our names, boat name, MMSI number, email, mobile and web address on MS Publisher, but it could easily be done on MS Word. We also added our boat logo, but you could also jazz it up with a photo. It proved invaluable. We decided not to put our home address on it because it does advertise the fact that you are away from home for an extended period if it was to fall into the wrong hands. One sailing couple created a bookmark with their contact details on it and those of the charity that they were raising money for.

PRESENTING YOUR TRIP

Once you have completed your circumnavigation, you may want to give a talk about your trip. You will then be presented with the challenge of compressing several months cruising into a limited time slot and reducing the number of photos to a manageable number. Here are some hints for preparing a professional presentation:

➤ Use MS Power Point with several photos with captions on a slide rather than one photo per page; this allows you to show more photos.
➤ Include several chartlets showing your track, it helps audiences visualise the area that you are talking about.
➤ Create a standard header for your slides, which is the same font and size on each slide.
➤ Don't make a slide too complicated; use a maximum of five photos.
➤ Work out the number of slides you need for the time slot you have. Allow approximately three minutes per slide.

A sample of our Power Point slide presentation.

➤ Print out the slides with space for Speakers' Notes (this is an A4 page with four miniature slides with room at the side to place your notes), write key bullet points of topics you want to mention. This allows you to see what slide is coming next.
➤ Practise: rehearse at least three times
➤ Do not face the screen when doing your presentation. It makes it difficult for your audience to hear you and they will just see your back.

A summary of communications equipment:

Computer	Phone	Writing	Camera
Computer	Mobile phone	Paper and memo pads	Camera
12V charger	12V charger	Envelopes	Camera battery charger
Printer		Stamps	Spare battery
Data card		Pens	Spare memory card
Paper			Film for non digital

10

NAVIGATION

In 1869, Empson Middleton was the first person to sail single-handed around England and Lowland Scotland via what is now called the Firth and Forth Canal – a voyage which he recounts in *The Cruise of the Kate*. This was a feat of endurance, because his engineless yacht's only form of propulsion, apart from the sails, were oars. The *Kate*, according to Lloyds Register, was a 25-foot wooden yacht with an iron keel; so Middleton would find himself rowing to the point of utter exhaustion to reach a harbour entrance or to round a headland, in order to beat an adverse tidal stream. Navigation provided its own challenges at that period. He describes passing through Hurst Narrows against the flood tide: 'I kept as close as I could to Hurst, feeling the depth as I went along with a boat hook, which is much handier than the lead.' He complains that the charts were drawn for the commercial coasters, so sometimes lacked some details: 'the headlands are not sufficiently defined; but, worse than that the bays are not properly indented.'

Thankfully, navigation today has become much simpler with the advent of GPS, chart plotters, radar and more accurate charts. However, that doesn't detract from the challenges and the sense of achievement when you have completed your trip. This cruise will test your navigation skills: strong tides, tidal gates, rocks, sand banks; all to be negotiated in varying degrees of visibility.

Of the 46 skippers whose qualifications were known, 52 per cent were qualified to at least practical RYA Yachtmaster™ Offshore level. This doesn't mean that you need this qualification to do the cruise; 48 per cent successfully completed the circumnavigation without it. Indeed six skippers had no qualifications but they had a great deal of experience. The important point is that you should have the knowledge that is covered by the Yachtmaster™ syllabus, backed up by practical sailing experience.

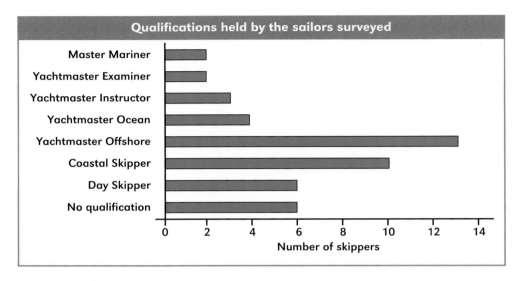

PUBLICATIONS
Almanacs

Almanacs are full of invaluable information. We used the loose-leaf *Reeds Almanac* rather than the individual area almanacs in order to reduce the cost. It was invaluable because of the incredible amount of detail contained within it. The main disadvantage, not surprisingly, is its size. Some suggestions to make it easier to use:

➤   Ditch all the countries that you won't be visiting, though if you have the Reeves Fowkes tidal atlases keep Cherbourg, as it is the standard port for the Channel.

➤   Take self-sticking plastic hole reinforcers or frequently-used pages will fall out.

➤   Laminate the key standard ports tidal information beforehand, so that the pages stand up to life on the chart table.

➤   Use stick on/Post-it type paper flags, so that key information in the Almanac is easier to find quickly; for example flag up the standard port you are using, the port you are entering and leaving, sunrise and sunset times.

Pilot books

Reeds Almanac could easily replace pilot books; there is excellent passage information around the major tidal gates, often better than some pilot books, which tend to focus on the harbours. However, pilot books provide photos which help when entering ports or anchorages, plus they help you to decide where to go.

The UK and Ireland is covered by seven *Admiralty Sailing Directions* which are aimed at providing essential navigational information for ocean-going vessels. The latest editions have good colour photos of the harbours, but they are not aimed at the leisure market, so lack information about small anchorages. They are listed in Appendix 2: At £46 (2007) they are an expensive option compared to the leisure pilot books which retail between £15 and £30. These provide valuable information and chartlets about entering anchorages and harbours. There are a large number of leisure pilot guides and many cover roughly the same areas. It is usually a matter of personal preference as to which you choose. There is one other book which is worth mentioning: David Rainsbury's *Fearsome Passages*; it provides some useful advice for many of the infamous stretches of water that you will meet on a circumnavigation of Britain.

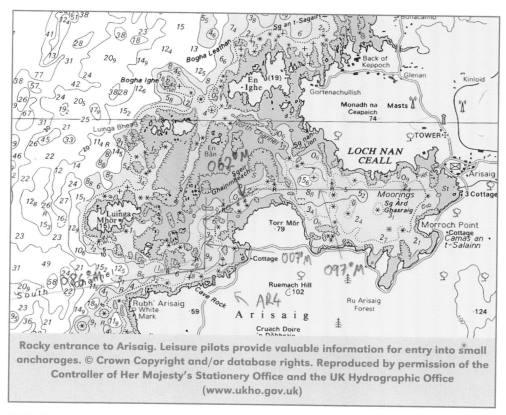

Rocky entrance to Arisaig. Leisure pilots provide valuable information for entry into small anchorages. © Crown Copyright and/or database rights. Reproduced by permission of the Controller of Her Majesty's Stationery Office and the UK Hydrographic Office (www.ukho.gov.uk)

Tidal atlases

We used a combination of Reeves Folkes and the Admiralty tidal atlases. We cut out the pages, laminated each one, and then bound them together with metal rings. Or you can get them wire-bound by an office supplier such as Staples. We then used indelible markers to write the times on the pages and nail varnish remover to clean them afterwards. This meant they didn't get into a soggy mess and will last for years!

Tides in the Orkneys and Shetland Islands Twice a day the tide surges from the Atlantic to the North Sea and back again, with the flow being concentrated by the archipelago of 170 islands that make up the Orkney and Shetland Islands. This results

The rewards of rock hopping
9th June – Tobermory to Arisaig

Topped up with fuel, as this was likely to be the last fuel stop for a while, we set off from Tobermory, but noticed that the rev counter was going haywire. So we headed back in and picked up a buoy again and checked out the alternator, which seemed fine. So we set off once more and it seemed to settle down. There was 20 knots of wind and we cruised along at 7 knots downwind, which was great, as we could make up the lost time. We rounded Ardnamurchan point – UK mainland's most westerly point, with the customary bunch of white heather tied to the pulpit. There was blue sky and a good wind – we were incredibly lucky. Arisaig has a difficult entrance, with very rocky outcrops and a winding route through – 'not for the faint hearted' as the pilot book says. It was tempting just to keep sailing and miss it out and go for an easier harbour. We decided to go for it and pick our way past the rocks and follow the poles. There were brilliant white beaches between the rocks surrounded by turquoise pools of water. We successfully navigated our way in under engine and felt very pleased with ourselves; then a boat the same size as ours sailed out – nothing like making us feel like amateurs! We had dinner in the cockpit and watched a stunning sunset over the Isles of Rum and Eigg – another amazing day.

in the strongest tides in the British Isles, and they can reach up to 12 knots. It is therefore no surprise that the Orkneys have been chosen for an experimental wave and tide power generation site. If you are just going through the Pentland Firth then the Admiralty tidal atlas *NP209* gives detailed tidal information. However, if you are planning to spend time in the Islands, then *NP209* does not give you enough information, as the arrows are too general, given the strengths of the tides. The excellent *Clyde Cruising Club (CCC) Sailing Directions for the north and north-east coasts of Scotland and Orkney Islands* provide local tidal rates and directions, to enable detailed planning. They have plotted the tidal information from the Admiralty charts. There is a separate *CCC Sailing Directions for the*

Sunset over Eigg and Rum from Arisaig

Shetland Islands. If you speak to any of the harbour masters in the area, they will give you information and advice about crossing the Pentland Firth.

The Orkneys were our favourite place on the trip, but do plan the tides carefully. For example, Eyenhallow Sound is meek at slack water, but as Orcadian Willie Tulloch, and the former Master of the Northern Lightvessel said to us 'it can be an evil piece of water'. We saw it at springs with a slight (F2) wind over tide and it looked positively scary ... and that was from the safety of the land.

Chart datums

By the end of 2008, all Admiralty charts for UK and Irish waters will be based on the same positional datum, WGS 84. Until then, when planning your route on a chart and then entering it into a chart plotter, you must ensure that the same datum is used. Most now use WGS 84 but you will still find some *Ordnance Survey of Great Britain 1936.* Imray charts are now all WGS 84.

ROUTE PLANNING

Although we had our route roughly planned out, there was the opportunity to deviate, provided we had the appropriate charts. The *Rough Guides* also helped us to decide where we wanted to go, in combination with the all-important *Almanac* and pilot guides. You will also get much invaluable information by talking to crews from other boats and to the locals. Much of your time is spent deciding what areas you will have to miss out.

Solas V regulations dictate prior passage planning and anybody considering this trip should plan each leg very careful. Clearly, everyone will have their own preferred format and method. We had a system using an A4 book to plan all routes. Using a double-page spread, one page set out the route's waypoints and one was used for logging tidal information, weather, radio channels, contingency ports, times to be at tidal gates etc.

We used our rest days to plan the waypoints for a couple of days in advance, plotting them together with the course on the chart and also setting up the route in the chart plotter. So if you arrive late, you can plan to continue

Across the Pentland Firth towards Duncansby Head

A healthy respect is needed for the rost in Eyenhallow Sound

the next day without needing to spend time course plotting during the evening. Make rough notes about tidal streams but leave the detailed tidal planning until you are certain of the day you are leaving, otherwise much time is wasted doing tidal calculations that are never used.

We used A4 white boards with indelible coloured marker pens to draw the harbour entrance or approaches to an anchorage with key infor-mation on it such as: lights and buoys, rocks, courses for entry and leaving, plus tidal heights expected at given times for anchoring. It proved to be a very useful system when exiting the meandering River Dee from Kirkcudbright at night with 26 different flashing red lights, ticking them off as we sailed along.

Planning software

If you are really organised, you can preplan many of your waypoints and routes before starting your cruise. Jonathan Hutchinson (*Zia Maria* Moody 31) set off with 276 essential or potentially useful waypoints and 30 pre-planned route segments, already loaded into his GPS, using planning software. We had planning software on our PC but because it didn't interface to our chart plotter, we didn't use it, as it would have meant the double entry of waypoints.

NIGHT SAILING

From our survey, we found that on average, most yachts only spent three full nights at sea; no motor boats spent a whole night at sea. However, there were many late nights and early starts. Whilst we only had two nights at sea, we did 44 night hours. If you are around the north of Scotland

Stromness at 11pm with Hoy in the background

in June, you will benefit from twilight all night (TAN); the sun does not reach an attitude of –12 degrees, so it never gets truly dark.

CHART PLOTTERS

The price of chart plotters has decreased dramatically, so the technology is now within the reach of most people. We installed a chart plotter by the chart table (12in screen) and a small chart plotter (7in screen) in the cockpit. A cheap deal on out-of-date equipment, bought at a boat show, allowed us to have this luxury. The chart plotter by the chart table was excellent for planning and also had a dual purpose as radar. It is angled so that the radar screen can be seen from the cockpit. It was the first time that I had used a chart plotter, as we fitted it specifically for this trip. Despite being brought up with traditional methods, I have to admit I appreciated it, particularly when we were negotiating the Scottish Islands, or were sailing in fog. It was a great advantage to be able to relate the chart directly to the landscape around you. It is important to check the chart plotter against the actual coastline to see that the information given makes sense, as with all electronic navigation aids, it is easy to get mesmerised.

Always plot the waypoints and route on your chart, as you never know when your electronic systems will fail. Ours did fail entering the Chanonry Narrows on the Moray Firth but as we had the course on the chart and on our white board, it was not a problem. Many boats now rely on chart plotters but you must plot your position regularly. We always made a manual plot every hour, and every 10 minutes in fog. We also had the radar linked to the chart plotter on deck.

Chart plotters are available either as software running on a computer (or laptop) or as a dedicated piece of equipment. The dedicated equipment tends to have lower power requirements than a computer. Even so, when on long passages, we tended to turn off the cockpit plotter to save power. Make sure that the chart plotter has a screen large enough to make it readable.

FORWARD-LOOKING ECHO SOUNDERS

A few years back, we met a couple who had been bluewater cruising for years and we asked them which was the single piece of equipment that they valued the most; their reply was 'a forward-looking echo sounder'. This gives you the ability to look ahead, as opposed to below the vessel. It can give you more confidence when exploring unfamiliar or poorly charted areas. Depending on your equipment, it displays two views of your underwater surroundings:

➤ *Horizontal scan* This displays a bird's eye view of your surroundings with depth differentiated by colour.
➤ *Vertical scan* This displays what is immediately in front of the boat's heading as a cross section of the ground. It doesn't provide visibility on either side of the boat's heading.

Most forward-looking echo sounders are only able to show the vertical scan and the advantage of these is that the transponder is small. We fitted a forward-looking echo sounder which has both scans; the disadvantage was the size of the transponder, which had the hydrodynamic properties of a bungalow. The horizontal view was the one that we used the most. It was extremely useful coming out of the River Dee one night, particularly as two of the navigation lights were not working. If you do fit one, be aware that it can create turbulence under your boat, which can affect your log readings. We fitted ours beyond the limit set on the instructions and it still affected our log, which we had to recalibrate. A forward-looking echo sounder was useful but was by no means an essential bit of equipment for this cruise and with hindsight (that exact science), I would not have fitted it.

ADDITIONAL NAVIGATION EQUIPMENT

We found the following items very useful:

General	
Dividers	Binoculars
Breton plotter	Hand-held compass
Pencils	Hand-held GPS (back up)
Eraser	Pens
Pencil sharpener	Route planning A4 book
Log book	Calculator
Hole reinforcers	2 A4 white boards
Post-it notes for flagging almanac	Nail polish remover
Admiralty symbols *5011*	Green, red, blue, black, purple indelible fine marker pens
Ruler	Map correction pen

11

LIFE ON BOARD

WATCHKEEPING

It always surprises me how many of skippers, when doing a long trip like crossing the Channel, will stay awake for the entire passage. If you try and do this on this cruise, you will end up shattered, and increase the likelihood of making unsafe decisions due to tiredness. You need to organise regular watchkeeping to pace yourself, so ensuring that you are adequately rested. Clearly, if you are single-handed this is not a luxury you have, so careful consideration must be given to length of legs and proper recovery time after a long leg.

For any passages over 4 hours, we set up a watch keeping routine. 3 hours on, 3 hours off during the day and 2 hours on, 2 hours off at night. Though at times this was flexible if the person on watch felt wide awake, they would often allow the 'off watch' to sleep an hour longer. For legs shorter than 4 hours, we used to do joint watches but we would always be clear as to whose watchkeeping responsibility it was. If there was fog and we were in an area where there was a lot of shipping or hazards, we would do joint watches.

It is important to set up good watchkeeping routines from day one:

➤ Brief the crew as to what to expect on the leg.
➤ Make sure they know when they should waken the skipper.
➤ Have a clear handover at change of watch.

SEASICKNESS

When the sea state goes from smooth to slight, Mags generally starts to be 'stomach aware' – the first stage of seasickness. For those fellow suffers, you will be pleased to know that you do get your sea legs. She managed to do the entire trip without being seasick, though there was the odd time when she felt grim. Here are her top tips:

➤ Minimise the amount of time that you need to perform tasks down below:
  ✦ Prepare lunch in advance before leaving the harbour.
  ✦ Use food flasks, which would be filled with hot food if sailing overnight and we were expecting a rough sea.
  ✦ Prior to a trip, we would fill a flask with boiling water. Our flask dispenses through a push button on top. This means that when you are heeling you don't have to defy gravity when filling up a cup, as you can take the cup to the flask and not the flask to the cup. This is very useful even if you don't suffer from seasickness.
➤ Use a combination of drugs plus sea bands.
➤ Keep warm.
➤ Pick your battles: if we knew there was going to be a rough sea, and we had enough time in our schedule to say in harbour, we did so.
➤ Keep a stack of ginger biscuits to nibble when you become stomach aware.
➤ Make sure you keep drinking.
➤ Take medication regularly as per the instructions.
➤ Part of the rationale for putting a chart plotter in the cockpit was to enable Mags to ensure that we were safe even if she was not prepared to venture down to the chart table below.

Every sufferer will have their preferred drugs. On board we took Stugeron and Scopoderm (Scopolamine) patches. The patches are invaluable because they can be administered even when you are unable to keep any food down.

EATING AND DRINKING

It is important to make sure that you eat and drink properly whilst at sea. It is easy to become dehydrated. The hot water flask, described above, meant that hot drinks were always readily available. Not only does it help to reduce the time spent below but it reduces the effort to have a hot drink, which means you are more like to have one. The quick tasty pasta meals that we carried also ensured that a hot dinner was always available no matter how late we arrived.

We kept a tupperware box in a cockpit locker filled with sweets and biscuits which helped to pass the night watch and gave a sugar boost to keep us awake. Though it is not good for the hips!

Mini flasks made by Life Adventure, which have screw-on tops, were invaluable. They would keep a cup of tea warm for a couple of hours. So if we were leaving in the early morning we could make cups of tea and enjoy a few sips at a time for the next couple of hours. Thermo mugs lost their heat by the time we had cast off the warps and were just out of the harbour.

Eating out

Our budget didn't stretch to eating out in restaurants, so we made do with the occasional treats of fish and chips and ice creams. Beware, you will come across lots of award winning fish and chip shops! We did conduct a national ice cream survey; the best was in Lossiemouth, from the Italian shop just opposite the old harbour. Fishermen's Missions provide excellent food, though sadly we missed out on the fish and chips in Kinlochbervie Mission, which were recommended to us by several happy customers. Be warned it closes at 2pm on a Friday.

If your budget does stretch to eating out, a guide book such as the *Rough Guide* comes into its own for recommending good eateries. However, in some places the choice can be limited; here is an example. We were in the tourist office of Kyle of Lochalsh, a village in Scotland with one main street whose claim to fame was that it used to be the departure point for the ferry to Skye, prior to the bridge being built. When a tourist asked the manager for a recommendation of a good restaurant. He explained 'being the Tourist Board we are not allowed to recommend any'. The tourist enquired 'can you tell me where the concentration of restaurants are'. After the manager stopped laughing, he replied 'if we have one of anything here we are lucky, let alone a concentration'.

ENTERTAINMENT

Socialising

We always made a point of inviting other sailors, moored near to us, over for drinks. We had some great evenings and made some good friends; this is one of the pleasures of cruising. However, according to one seasoned sailor we met, it was, surprisingly, quite rare to be invited over for drinks; he said people tended to stay on their boats.

On several occasions, we pooled our food with neighbouring boats and had a slap-up feast. Socialising is also a good way of finding out about places to visit. We also invited local people on board for a drink if they were interested in our boat. After one such occasion, we were then invited back for a meal at their home.

Games

Take along some games to pass the evenings: travel scrabble and backgammon occupied the odd hour for us. Two boat crews we surveyed took along golf clubs, one anchoring off St Andrews to make a quick trip ashore for a round at the home of golf.

Watching wildlife

One of the highlights on our trip was being able to see wildlife at such close quarters. I now realise that our normal cruising ground, on the south coast of England, is relatively devoid of wildlife in comparison to the rest of the UK waters. So a book on birdlife and mammals of the sea is essential to help with identification.

The bird life was plentiful and a few were our companions: Fulmars seemed to love playing chicken with the forestay; razorbills did a very good impressions of penguins, guillemots would fly in formation and always looked purposeful. When we got further north, skuas and great skuas appeared. These large sinister-looking birds are the bullies of the air, chasing other birds until their victims vomit up their food through sheer exhaustion, which the skua then eats. A special mention should go to the comical puffins, who appear to have missed out on the skills of landing on land and water. As they approach, they lower their orange feet, which

Puffins at Westray taken at 11pm without a flash and not using a zoom – he was that close!

have the aerodynamic properties of blocks of concrete, resulting in a crash landing. You will see them on the water, but you will rarely get a photo of them; they dive just as you get your camera ready. However, if you visit Westray (Orkneys), ask the harbour master about the puffins roosting site at Castle O'Burrian and you will see them landing two feet away from you as they come into to roost at dusk.

In anchorages, we would suddenly realise we were being watched by two big brown eyes, as an inquisitive seal had popped up. Then there were the dolphins and porpoises, which make everyone smile. They love to play in your bow wave and they genuinely seem interested in watching you when they surface. On one night watch, Mags heard a wave breaking and was convinced we were about to hit something but it turned out to be dolphins. She was then treated to a spectacular display, with the phosphorescence illuminating their tracks, as they sped around the boat like friendly torpedoes. It was like a Disney film, with sparkles following their twists and turns.

Basking sharks are occasionally seen, though one couple reported seeing 25 off the coast near Padstow. Several boats reported seeing whales en route: minke and orca. If you are very lucky you may see a giant turtle; they have been spotted off the Dingle Peninsula, on the west coast of Ireland.

Diving

Several crews went diving en route. All credit to Sarah Fagg (*Huffin*, Hurley 22) and her stowing abilities – she sailed around Britain via Cape Wrath, and managed to fit two full sets of diving kit in a 22ft yacht and had room for another crew member!

DVDs

We bought a few DVDs on eBay prior to the trip; they were well worth it, especially as we then sold them on return, for more than we paid.

Top: Warkworth Castle, near Amble.
Right: Skara Brae, Orkney – perhaps inspiration for the
first version of IKEA's flat pack furniture.

Memberships

We decided that being a member of the National Trust would be a good thing for the trip, allowing access free of charge. Sadly all buildings and monuments we wanted to visit belonged either to English or Scottish Heritage. Membership of one of these organisations would have saved us money.

Books

Swapping books is a good way to keep your library refreshed. A few marinas had book swaps. Puzzle books are always good to while away the hours when storm bound if you like that sort of thing.

Radio

We didn't miss the TV but we listened to the radio a great deal. Radio 4 afternoon plays became compulsory listening. Being an avid Archers fan, my highlight was a cracking good sail listening to the omnibus of the Archers. Sad I know!

SHOWER FACILITIES

We were generally able to get a shower either at the harbour facilities, youth hostels or Fishermen's Missions. At Kinlochbervie, we had to decide between a shower or the infamous fish and chips, as we arrived just as it was about to close. However, they did stay open longer, to allow us to get our shower; an example of one of the many kindnesses that we experienced en route. To improve your showering experience in marina and municipal showers, take a shower mat with you. Also a pair of flip flops minimises the contact your feet have with the floors, which can at times be somewhat unpleasant.

The best shower facility award has to go to Crinan Canal (the landing stage at Bellanoch Bridge). Here we had our own private shower and loo in a former lock keeper's building and, like all things on the canal, it was immaculate. A special mention should go to Amble Marina which has a bath as part of the facilities; 50p buys you enough hot water for a reasonable bath, a £1 gets you enough water for a total soak, and it was sheer luxury.

The worst facility award has to go Inverness Harbour (Longmans) mainly because there was only the use of a disgusting loo during office hours and there were no shower facilities. However, the lack of facilities was not reflected in the price. If you arrive outside the sea lock opening hours, which are determined by high water or like us, not entering the canal, you may need to use this facility. However, a new marina in Inverness is opening in 2008.

KEEPING A HAPPY SHIP

A trip like this should be an experience of a lifetime, one to treasure, especially if you are a couple. If you and your crew are to make a success of the cruise, a good atmosphere is vitally important. Sailing together worked really well for us, so we decided to look in detail at why it worked:

➤ Don't embark on this trip unless you and your crew already get on well with each other ashore.

➤ There is only one skipper on a boat, so it is important to designate a skipper who has ultimate responsibility

➤ Good communications are essential to prevent misunderstandings and frustration building up. It is also important to share concerns and not let them bottle up. I can at times be too risk averse when in a harbour. The longer I am storm bound, the more apprehensive I seem to get. Mags was always a good sounding board to bring me back to reality.

➤ Play to your strengths and split the tasks based on what you enjoy and are usually more skilled at, rather than on gender-related lines. I never understand why men always tend to drive the boat when anchoring and leave the woman to manhandle the anchor, despite the man usually being the stronger of the two. Being two women, we weren't bound by boy jobs and girl jobs! Even though we had our preferred tasks, we still knew how to do each other's task, as a back up.

➤ Ensure that you plan everything together, so that both have an equal say in the important decisions. You may have one skipper but it is joint ownership of the cruise that makes it a success. This doesn't stop you splitting the tasks in order to make best use of time. This holds true for both pre-trip planning and during the cruise.

➤ Whilst I am the skipper and hold the Yachtmaster Offshore qualification, I had confidence in Mags' ability as a Day Skipper to run a watch without me. She also

Looking down the Kyle of Loch Alsh

knows her limitations and knows when to call me and ask for advice when I was off watch. I know of many crews where their skipper very rarely went to sleep. The superman concept will lead to exhaustion.

➤ If you are responsible for one task, then make sure the other crew is kept informed. For example, I would do the detailed route planning and then would brief Mags on the planning, the logic, tidal gates etc.

➤ Common tasks are a good way of building a strong team. We would carry out joint pilotage coming into harbours; not only is it a good sanity check but it also gave us a joint sense of achievement. In fog, or close to hazards, I would be up on deck and Mags would man the radar.

➤ Understand each other's weaknesses and be prepared to compromise. I am not very good at relaxing, so I am always busy doing things, tweaking sails, helming. Mags can easily switch off and would happily set the sails, the autohelm and do a puzzle book on watch, looking up regularly, of course, to keep watch. There was no point in me getting anxious that we were not going as fast as we possibly could; it wasn't a race.

➤ The trip is a challenge and will be hard work so you need commonly agreed goals. If your goals are different from the start, then it will not be a rewarding challenge. I mentioned this in the introduction but can't stress this enough. So spend time getting a common understanding of what you want to achieve to make this trip memorable.

SAILING WITH CHILDREN

This trip can be a rich and rewarding adventure, with real quality time for any family. For those who have read Libby Purves excellent book *One Summer's Grace* will also know that it can also have its challenges. Greg and Sue Hill (*Blue Argolis* Trewes 41) completed the trip via Cape Wrath during the summer holidays with their children Kate and Sebastian (10 and 12 respectively). Whilst much depends on your children (and you know them best), they offered the following advice:

➤ Too much time spent at sea can be boring for children, so make sure that you have allowed for enough shore days and that you plan your route to have fun activities ashore. 'London and St Katherine's Dock was a great hit, how else can a family of four stay in the centre of London for £40'. Too many deserted anchorages will not give the children a chance to get ashore easily or the opportunity to meet children from other boats.

➤ Have confidence in your own abilities and those of your mate.

➤ Involve the children in activities: navigation, watch keeping etc.

Here is some advice from Mike and Michelle Perry (*Caribbean Breeze* Fairline 36 Turbo), who completed a circumnavigation round Britain via the Caledonian Canal, with their children Letitia and Michael Perry (10 and 9 respectively) also in the school holidays:

➤ A television with a video/DVD can be quite a boon for young children.

➤ Impose strict rules about the wearing of lifejackets whenever the kids were outside, whether at sea or not.

➤ Be tolerant of their needs and wishes.

A memorable day's sail
14 June Kyleakin to Loch Gairloch

We set off at a civilised time (8.30am) and passed under the controversial bridge to Skye. Behind which was the most sublime view of Loch Alsh and the surrounding mountains, which appeared as layers on a canvas, with each layer of mountains being a different colour, lightening as they regressed into the background. Despite the gloomy forecast, it was actually a lovely warm day and we donned our shorts. We headed northwards, up the Inner Sound and on the way saw dolphins, puffins (who managed to evade Mags' 500 attempts to capture them on camera) and seals. It was blowing about F2, we had the cruising chute up as we glided along at a gentle pace up the length of Skye, with the Cuillins framing the backdrop behind us. We arrived early in Loch Gairloch, which allowed us time to explore the area and we walked up to some local waterfalls. We decided to treat ourselves and go to the local pub for a meal (the first meal out of the trip). It was another excellent day ... one of many.

YOUR BOAT WILL BE YOUR HOME

One of the greatest compliments we receive is when people come on board and they say how homely it is. Extended cruising doesn't need to mean really basic conditions. We cruised in comfort by adding a few extras, it does increase the weight, but as our boat is already eight tonnes in the water, we can live with a little more:

➤ A picture on the wall and scatter cushions (made of fire retardant material) give a homely feel to the saloon. We ban anyone from sitting on saloon cushions wearing sailing clothing, because once you have salt on your cushions, they will just absorb water and you will always have that damp feeling in the fabric.

➤ Proper china mugs and plates (they never broke) made us feel that we weren't camping. Though we did have plastic bowls with lids for when eating at sea. We used the lids for plates for lunch at sea.

➤ Proper glasses for wine and the odd dram; again we have plastic ones for use at sea.

➤ Proper bedding such as a duvet, sheet and memory foam mattress can make a bunk seem civilised. We had sleeping bags that we used when at sea.

➤ Scented nappy sacks to place your used loo paper in.

FLAGS

En route you will have the opportunity to fly several flags, some of which you might want to buy in advance:

➤ *Courtesy flags* Depending on your route and nationality you may need the Irish or British courtesy flag. You may also like to consider optional courtesy flags: for example, Scottish Saltire or regional flags such as Orkneys, Devon, Cornwall.

➤ *Q flag* If you are from the European Union then no Q flag is required, as both Ireland and the UK are in the EU (unless visiting the Channel Islands).

Dressing overall

This trip is a great excuse to dress overall, either at the beginning or end of the cruise. Note that it is much easier to fly the flags if you have sewn them onto a 5 or 6mm line or buy them made up. The flag order is as follows:

From the bow: E, Q, p3, G, p8, Z, p4, W, p6, P, p1, I, Code, T, Y ,B, X, 1st Sub, H, 3rd Sub, D, F, 2nd Sub, U, A, O, M, R, p2, J, p0, N, p9, K, p7, V, p5, L, C, S. The size of flags should be appropriate to the size of the boat and for a single masted boat the break at the mast should come between the 3rd substitute and the D.

13

SAFETY

Thankfully, accidents involving the loss of life at sea, seldom happen, so it is easy to become complacent. On the last day of our cruise, we heard the Mayday call during the search, to the south of the Isle of Wight, for the yacht *Ouzo* and her crewmembers. A Marine Accident Investigation concluded that the *Ouzo* had been in collision with a cross-Channel passenger ferry, resulting in the tragic deaths of the three crew. This is a grim reminder of how important safety afloat is – especially with regard to watchkeeping.

The aim should be to minimise the chance of an incident happening; but if it does, then to make sure you and your crew have the skills and equipment to deal with it. This is particularly important on a circumnavigation; whilst you may never be too far from land, much of the coast is remote and far from civilisation. Therefore you should treat this as an offshore cruise, as opposed to a coastal one, when selecting your equipment. Prior to your trip, try to attend the RYA Sea Survival course, if you haven't already done so. Not only because of the invaluable information that you learn about emergency situations but also, you can discuss the merits of different types of safety equipment. A good course provider will have examples on show of all the different types of safety equipment and will know the advantages and disadvantages of each.

Righting a liferaft

EMERGENCY SITUATIONS AND EQUIPMENT

We considered all the risks and then planned what safety equipment we would need to have on board. It is also a balance between cost and the space that you have available onboard. The good news is that you should have many of these items already. This was our list:

Emergency situation	Equipment	Location/comment
Man overboard	Lifejackets fitted with lights, hoods, crotch straps and integrated harness. Automatic release	Worn
	MOB block and tackle recovery system	Wet locker
	Long swim ladder (reaching 0.5m below water line)	Cockpit locker
	Danbuoy with light	Cockpit
	Life ring	Cockpit
	Throwing line	Cockpit
	Life Sling	Pushpit
	Mini flares	In pocket during watch, attach a lanyard to the firing pin
Abandon ship	Liferaft in canister	Foredeck
	Grab bag in floating waterproof container	Companionway. It has a mini drogue on it
	RORC flares in floating waterproof container	Companionway. It has a mini drogue on it
	Water in floating container	Companionway
	EPIRB 406Hz	Companionway
Fire	Engine fire extinguisher	Engine compartment
	Powder fire extinguishers	2kg: saloon. 1kg: aft cabin, forepeak, cockpit locker
	Fire blanket	Near galley and aft cabin, as no secondary escape from the aft cabin
	Smoke and gas detector	Aft cabin
Collision	Sea-me active radar reflector	
	3 bilge pumps	1 operated below deck, 1 operated above deck and 1 for emergency use.
	White flares	Companionway reachable from cockpit
	Steamer scarer	Cockpit - plugged in when on night watches
	Hole repair kit	Below decks but above water line
Loss of rig	Shootit gas-powered wire cutter	Companionway
	Bolt cutters	Behind companionway steps

Emergency situation	Equipment	Location/comment
Loss of rig	Emergency radar reflector	Chart table
	Emergency antenna	Chart table
Fouled propeller	Full diving suit including hood, gloves, boots, mask, waterproof torch, fins and snorkel	In locker below deck
	Rope cutter	On shaft by propeller
	Folding propeller	Main propeller on shaft
Electrical failure	Emergency navigation lights	Companionway
	Handheld VHF radio	Below deck in grab bag
	Handheld GPS	Chart table
Loss of steering	Emergency steering	Cockpit locker
Seacock failure	Sea cock plugs (tapered wooden plugs) that fit into the seacock in case of failure	Attached by lanyard to the seacock, so it is ready to use
Rope wrapped round limb	Emergency knife	In protective cover in mast halyard bag
General	DSC radio	
	Laminated Mayday procedure	Near the radio

Emergency Position Indicating Radio Beacon (EPIRB)

The EPIRB when activated allows the rescue co-ordination centre to find your boat in an emergency, by sending off a distress signal via the COPAS/SARSAT satellites. There are several differences between types of EPIRBs: the accuracy which determines the size of search area and time to the detect signal:

121.5MHz beacon	12.5nm radius: 490 sq miles area Up to 6 hours for signal to be picked up
406MHz beacon	3nm radius: 28 sq miles area Approximately 1-2 hours for signal to be picked up
406MHz beacon with GPS	0.1nm radius: 0.03 sq miles area Under 30 minutes for signal to be picked up

Due to many false alerts and poor detection, the 121.5MHz will be phased out in 2009. However, the other beacons will still retain a signal 121.5MHz which allows rescue boats and helicopters to home in on the signal. There is a cheaper version that allows your EPIRB to interface to your ship's GPS. It is important to register 406MHz beacons to ensure that a search operation is initiated when the EPIRB is activated.

There are also differences between how EPIRBs are released: Category 1 EPIRBs float free and switch on automatically. Category 2 is deployed manually but still can be activated by water, once it has been freed from the bracket. EPIRBs are battery operated and they have a 3–5 year life; they usually operate for 48 hours once activated. As they contain internal batteries you will need to ensure that they do not need replacing during your trip.

Search And Rescue Transponder (SART)

Although we did not carry a SART, you may consider having one. This is a radar transceiver, which transmits a distinctive emergency signal that any ship can pick up on their radar. At long range, this signal is a stream of 12 in-line dots, turning to arcs at one mile and concentric circles at closer range. The advantage is that they can also be picked up by other vessels, rather than just the search and rescue craft.

Liferaft

You should not undertake this trip without a liferaft. You can either buy or rent one for the period. The RYA Sea Survival course allows you to practise getting in and out of one, and once dressed in full kit with a lifejacket, it makes you really appreciate what you are looking for in a liferaft.

The tragic end to the 1979 Fastnet race, where 15 yachtsmen drowned and the 1998 Sydney to Hobart Race, where a further 6 yachtsmen lost their lives, has resulted in the long awaited ISO 9650 standard. The route to this followed an Offshore Racing Council (ORC) standard, then the International Sailing Federation (ISAF) standard in 2003, then finally ISO 9650 (part 1 type 1 group A) which harmonises standards across Europe. Type 1 (group A) liferafts are designed for open ocean and ideal for long distance cruising, offshore voyages and racing yachts. There is a SOLAS standard but these are really only suitable for commercial vessels. The new standards have led to improvements, such as: boarding ladders, drogues, ballast pockets and strength of materials. You can upgrade your liferaft by the addition of different SOLAS packs either A (Offshore) or B (Coastal). Many of the newer liferafts have servicing intervals of every three years, as opposed to annually, which can help in the justification for upgrading to a newer model.

Your liferaft should be stowed where it is easily accessible and protected from heavy weather. You can choose to have your liferaft released automatically using a hydro-static release unit (HRU) which activates when submerged under 1–4m water; the liferaft will then float to the surface.

Loss of rig

Cutting through wire rigging is extremely difficult in calm conditions, let alone at sea in a storm. Neither of us felt confident about being able to cut rigging with just a pair of bolt cutters. Therefore we decided to buy the gas-powered Shootit, which cuts the wire once the trigger is pushed.

Man overboard – prevention is better than cure

As you will read in the log entry in the next chapter, Mags had to go into the water to cut off a rope from our propeller. Even in a wetsuit, the cold made her breathing difficult, and after 15 minutes in the water, getting back on the boat unaided was a real effort. Most people who do this trip, like us, are short-handed. One person has to be able to stop the boat, throw over danbuoys etc, press the MOB button, all whilst keeping an eye on the location of the casualty and then get the person back on board. All this reinforced our view that the best way to handle a MOB situation, was to *stay on board*. A single-hander has little chance of rescue, so staying on board is imperative. This should reinforce your decisions about when you should clip on. You may also consider a transom ladder, which can be released from sea level.

Make sure that you have planned and tested how you will get someone back on board, as they are unlikely to be able to help you.

You should try and support the casualty horizontally when you lift them from the water. If you lift them vertically out of the water, the blood drains from the head and a rapid drop in blood pressure can result in a heart attack. Systems such as the Jon Buoy are designed to keep the casualty in a horizontal position. If you are in a motor boat, you will not have the height to rig up a recovery system such as the one above. You may consider fitting a mini crane, which is the advice of Malcolm and Glenda Stennett (*Lady Genevieve* Broom 39). If not, you will need to use the bathing platform or the tender, if the sea is not rough. It is recommended to have a long line attached at one end to a stanchion and the other to an electric windlass, via a strong point such as a cleat. Winding the windlass should raise the casualty. This assumes that the casualty can help themselves, by standing straight on the line.

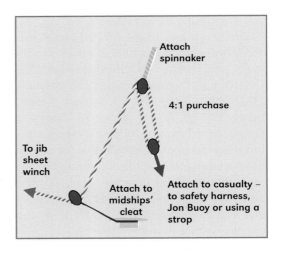

One fear, if there are just two of you onboard, is how would the off watch person know if you have gone overboard, especially if they are asleep? There are several options:

➤ *Low tech solution* Set an alarm every 15 minutes and the person on watch must reset the alarm before it sounds.
➤ *High tech solution* There are several electronic systems such as Raymarine LifeTag and Mobi-lert which will set off an alarm if you fall outside the guard zone of the base unit. Your position, when the signal is lost, is then recorded or plotted on the chart plotter. Our next investment will be one of these systems.

Grab bag

Your grab bag needs to reflect that you will be in colder climes but that you are not expected to be at sea for an unlimited time. Also take into account what you already have in your liferaft. We planned ours to save two people for two days. In an ideal world, you would have absolutely everything ready in your grab bag, though this would mean that you would have to have duplicate items eg EPIRB and handheld VHF radio. However, budget and space are limiting factors. So we had a spare dry bag kept next to the grab bag for additional items. We had a laminated list of all these items, also kept next to the grab bag:

	Item	Grab bag	Flare bag	Additional items	Water bag
Communications	Handheld VHF			●	
	VHF battery holder and spare batteries	●			
	Waterproof bag for VHF	●			
	RORC flare pack and welding glove		●		
	Whistle	●			
	Strobe light	●			
	Signal mirror	●			
	Fog horn			●	
	EPIRB			●	
	Emergency radar reflector			●	
Rations	Water (3 litres)				●
	Snap light stick (2)	●			
	Cereal bars, chocolate bars	●			
	Small plastic drinking bottle	●			
Clothing	Fleece hat (2)	●			
	Gloves (2 pairs)	●			
	Spare clothing			●	
Medical	First aid kit			●	
	Survival blanket	●			
	Petroleum jelly	●			
	Sun burn cream	●			
	Seasickness tablets and seasickness bags	●			

General				
	Hand warmers (8 chemical heat packs)	●		
	Plastic bags	●		
	Waterproof torch and spare batteries	●		
	Safety knife with blunt end and cutting board	●		
	Nylon string and duct tape	●		
	Camera in waterproof box		●	
	Compass		●	
	The *Grab Bag Book* (see book reference)	●		
	Credit card/money/yacht papers		●	

Make sure that once you pack your grab bag that it floats. In the liferaft, we had such items as: sea anchor, hand air pump, paddles, bailer and sponges. Check that the glue in your repair kit is suitable for use in a damp environment – some aren't! If not, include swimming pool glue.

Flares

Ensure that your flares are easy to access and that you know how to use them without having to read the instructions; you may need to use them at night. Hand-held flares become very hot when they are burning, therefore you should carry a pair of welding gloves to protect your hand.

Lifejacket

There are several decisions to be made about lifejackets:

➤ *How do they inflate?* There are several options: manual (pulling a lanyard), auto release (on contact with water) and hydrostatic release (releases on water pressure). Always check the condition of the gas cylinder and inflation system.

➤ *What buoyancy?* We made the mistake of buying 275N (Newton) lifejackets thinking that the extra buoyancy would make them safer. However, during a test in a swimming pool they nearly killed us; it was impossible to breath in them and so we needed to let out air. Jackets of 275N are designed for people wearing heavy equipment; hence the extra buoyancy is required. We should have used 150N jackets.

➤ *What features should the lifejacket have?* A lifejacket hood is essential for keeping the spray and water off your face if you are in the water. The best hoods are those already fitted. We purchased hoods that were stored in a pouch. When we come to replace our lifejackets, we will choose those with integrated hoods. A light should also be fitted. Fit and use crotch straps to prevent your lifejacket riding up.

➤ *When should you wear a lifejacket?* This is subject to much debate and you need to decide this for yourselves. Unless of course you are in Irish waters, where it is compulsory to wear lifejackets in all vessels larger than 7m. We chose to wear them all the time, whilst at sea.

➤ *Is it comfortable?* You will be wearing your lifejacket for long periods of time, so do make sure it is comfortable.

Lee cloths

You should have adequate passage-making berths on board with lee cloths to enable you to defy gravity whilst sleeping.

Boat rules

If you were to do a risk assessment, you probably would never leave the harbour. However, considering the worst things that can happen, then developing routines to reduce the likelihood of them occurring is a sound approach. Our boat rules were:

➤ Store all flammable liquids in sealed lockers in the cockpit, so they could not leak into the bilge.
➤ Heave-to when reefing. You then have a stable platform to work on.
➤ Wear oilskin bottoms when cooking at sea.
➤ Clip on in winds above 14 knots during the day, always at night or any time when you deem it necessary.
➤ Always wear a life jacket.
➤ When manually handling the anchor or anchor chain, disconnect the remote control so that it could not be accidentally pushed or stood on.
➤ Don't hang fenders from the guard rails for any length of time; attach them to a strong point: eg stanchion base, cleat or shroud.
➤ No rings to be worn at sea.
➤ When going up the mast always wear a safety harness and clip on.
➤ Rig up the steamer scarer light in the cockpit during night hours.

COASTGUARD

We would register our passage plan with the local Coastguard. If you have completed a CG 66 form in advance, which is their voluntary safety boat identification scheme, it will make registering your passage quicker. The forms are available from any Coastguard, MCA Marine Office, RNLI boathouse or online at www.mcga.gov.uk.

We normally sail on the south coast, where, during weekends, the local Solent Coastguard become totally fed up with leisure craft requesting radio checks every two minutes. However, elsewhere the Coastguard have more time and by radioing in daily, they get to know you, asking what you are doing and are very helpful and friendly. At one point we had a problem with our VHF signal strength, which was very low. The Coastguard were very helpful, switching to several different aerials to see if they could pick us up. It was with some regret that we would sign off from one Coastguard, but excitement when we first picked up the next one. Use *Reeds Almanac* or Admiralty Maritime Communications (NP 291 or NP 289) to find out the VHF channel for the Coastguard aerial in your location.

FOG

Whilst the gales reduce in the summer, the likelihood of fog increases as the warm moist air meets the colder sea. We encountered fog on 10 days during our trip; it is inevitable. Therefore you need the equipment to be able to make passage safely in such conditions. The key is to be seen and to see others.

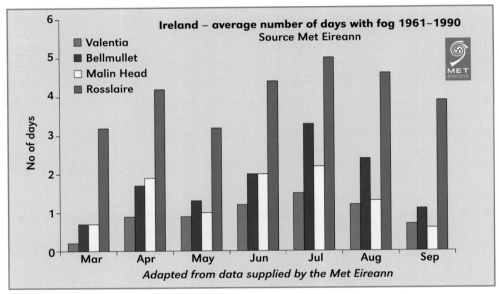

Adapted from data supplied by the Met Eireann

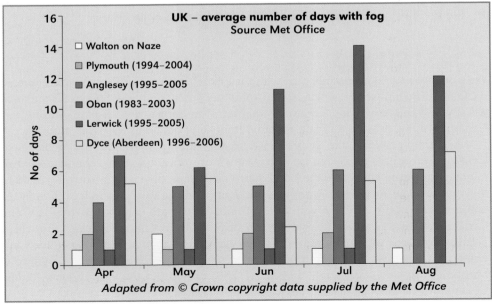

Adapted from © Crown copyright data supplied by the Met Office

Being seen

Plastic, GRP or wooden boats don't show up well on radar, therefore to be seen you need to improve your radar visibility. For boats under 15m, SOLAS V guidance for recreational craft requires that you to fit the largest radar reflector you can, as high as possible and to the manufacturer's instructions. Your visibility on radar is measured in two ways: radar cross section (RCS) and detection probability. Both need to be as large as possible. There is a current international standard ISO 8729 specification [1] which describes the required performance and there is a draft of the future standard ISO 8729 Ed 2.

If you have the chance to cruise in company on a lumpy sea with another boat that has radar, ask them at what range they lose you as a target; it can be quite scary. However, it is not as simple as just mounting a reflector and checking your visibility with another boat. It is even more difficult for commercial vessels to see recreational vessels due to the following reasons:

➤ The differences between leisure and commercial radars give them different detection abilities. The technical differences are around the angle of sea clutter zone and the angle of beam width. Radar visibility is also affected by the height of the other vessels' antennae – a yacht and a ferry have different heights of antennae.

➤ Marine radars operate on two bands: X-band and S-band. S-band improves the detection of large targets in bad weather and so requires a large scanner with higher power requirements, so is only fitted to large vessels. X-band is heavily affected by sea or rain clutter but has smaller scanner and power requirement, hence this is fitted to recreational boats. Large ships use both X- and S-bands, depending on the density of traffic and the sea state. There is no reflector available for recreational boats that operates effectively on S-band. Passive radar reflectors for recreational boats only offers a $\frac{1}{10}$th of the performance on S-band compared to that seen on X-band.

➤ For a large vessel to pick up and track a ship on an Automatic Radar Plotting Aid (ARPA), it is not just the maximum size of the peak that is important but also the consistency of the return echo at different bearings. Too many zero readings and it will not be tracked. For this reason, the new international standard recognises that the consistency of the response is more effective in raising the probability of detection than single peaks, and is defined as the stated performance level (SPL). The response has to be maintained at 10° (for motor cruisers and sailing vessels such as catamarans with a small angle of heel) and 20° (for all other sailing vessels).

➤ The performance of radar reflectors from different manufacturers varies greatly, with cost not necessarily being an indicator of effectiveness. Some performance has not matched the manufacturers' claims. A report commissioned by the Marine Accident Investigation Branch (MAIB), as a result of the loss of the *Ouzo* has provided an independent assessment of the most popular radar reflectors, comparing them to the current and future ISO standard. This along with other studies helps to inform recreational boaters which is the most effective and appropriate. However, it advises 'in certain circumstances their craft may still not be readily visible on ships' radars and thus they should always navigate with caution' (Report by QinetiQ Performance Investigation of Marine Radar Reflectors on the Market'). The report is available from the MAIB or on their website www.maib.gov.uk.

Combine these issues with the pitching and angle of heel and it is important that you do everything possible to make yourself seen and always be aware of the limitations of your system. You may consider doing an 'All ships' call when in fog. We were crossing the Pentland Firth in fog with radar and a Sea-Me active radar reflector fitted. Due to the nature of this stretch of water, all large vessels passing through have to radio into the Coastguard. Two vessels radioed in; normally you don't get the luxury of knowing what is out there beyond your ship's radar range. We took the decision to contact the two vessels to check they could see us. Thankfully they could, which was reassuring.

There are two types of radar reflector:

Active radar reflector This is a reflector which enhances a radar signal and then retransmits it when it receives it. This increases the detection range, and the chance that you will be seen. This results in a stronger signal around the full 360° azimuth. The Sea-Me is an example of an active reflector; it exceeds the requirement of both standards up to an angle of heel of 15°. It was recommended by the MAIB report if power was available; though it has some draw backs:

➤ A current draw of 350mA when transmitting and 150mA on standby.
➤ Only operates on X-band with no performance on S-Band.

Passive radar reflector The performance of this type varies greatly, from those considered not suitable, to higher end performers which just fail the two standards. The MAIB report makes essential reading when selecting a passive reflector.

Seeing others

It is also important to see others and not just rely on them seeing you. There are several options, which all have strengths and weaknesses.

Radar It is strongly recommended to have radar onboard for this trip, to allow you to make safe passage, either using a stand-alone radar or integrated with a chart plotter. To use radar safely, you need to do radar plots at regular intervals when you have detected other vessels.

Mini automatic radar plotting aid (MARPA) Technology has now made assessing the course of other targets easier. If your radar is fitted with this, it calculates the speed, course and closest point of approach of acquired targets. However, as it is based on radar, its accuracy can be affected by the boat's pitching and yawing. It is worth testing it on boats in good visibility to see this effect. So be aware of its limitations and use such features as electronic bearing lines (EBL) to track a vessel's course.

Automatic identification system (AIS) There is another system called AIS which allows you to be seen and see others who have AIS equipment fitted. All passenger vessels and commercial vessels over 300 tons are required, by law, to have an AIS installed. This equipment transmits key data every couple of seconds, such as the ship's name, MMSI number, position, speed, course and heading. This enables other vessels and port authorities to understand the movement of ships in their area. Some of the data is dynamic, so it is updated automatically and some has to be entered manually, eg destination. Yachts and motor boats have no legal requirement to have this system fitted but you can benefit from this technology if you choose to have the appropriate equipment fitted.

Transmitting AIS data To transmit data, an AIS transponder is required and there are two types of transponders:

➤ *Class-A AIS transponder for those vessels legally required to carry AIS equipment.* The frequency of data transmission depends on the speed of the vessel. Over 23 knots it is updated every 2 seconds, and less than 10 knots it is every 14 seconds.
➤ *Class-B AIS transponder designed for leisure craft and vessels that are not legally required to carry AIS equipment.* This device has the same features as the basic AIS receiver, plus the capability of being able to transmit your vessel's data as well, which it does every 30 seconds.

Any other AIS-equipped vessel within range will be able to identify your vessel on their AIS system. On large vessels and commercial ships, where the AIS system is fully integrated to their navigation systems, an automatic alarm should sound if a potential collision situation is detected, thus enabling the Watch Officers to take appropriate action to prevent a dangerous situation developing.

Receiving AIS data To receive the data, you need to have an AIS receiver. This will give you the ability to receive data but will not transmit your own boat's data. This information can be displayed either by:

➤ AIS receiver which is interfaced with a PC-based charting software or a compatible chart plotter. You are able to monitor the positions and movements of any other AIS-equipped vessel. The range is limited by that of the electronic charting display.
➤ Stand-alone AIS receiver which displays the positions and movements of AIS-equipped vessels on a simple LCD screen, similar to a radar display. Your vessel is located at the centre of the screen and you can zoom in or out, to locate any AIS-equipped vessels at different ranges.

Limitations to AIS In theory, AIS has the advantage over radar in that it provides accurate data which is not affected by the movement of the boat. However there are several limitations:

➤ It only works if vessels have the appropriate receiver and transponder, therefore it should not be regarded as a system that replaces radar.
➤ Some of the data is entered manually; therefore it is only as accurate as the operator.
➤ The heading on class A sets comes from the ship's compass and has proved to be unreliable at times.
➤ AIS is integrated to the ship's displays only on ships built after July 2008, so often on older ships it is difficult to see targets or the equipment can only handle a limited number.
➤ It operates on VHF band and class B does not have the same priority of data transmission as class A, which means that sometimes it doesn't transmit. Therefore, having a class B transponder is no guarantee that larger vessels have spotted you.

DINGHY SAFETY

It is easy to invest time and money in safety equipment and routines for your boat, and then hop into your dinghy and cross open water with little thought about safety. Some key points to staying safe in a dinghy:

➤ Always wear a lifejacket; we used to padlock them in the dinghy once ashore, to avoid having to carry them around.
➤ Don't overload the dinghy.
➤ Carry a handheld VHF radio; or carry mini flares if you are in an area of poor VHF coverage.
➤ Don't use a dinghy during periods of strong tidal flow; your outboard could fail and you will then be at the mercy of the tide.
➤ Always take oars with you.
➤ Secure your dinghy well above the tidal level on a rising tide. We saw a dinghy blow away in Holy Island due to this. The owner had used the dinghy, when there was a tide of 2.3 knots.
➤ Always carry spare fuel with you.

Dinghies recycled on Holy Island

13

HAZARDS IN COASTAL WATERS

POTS AND NETS

Virtually half of the 38 people surveyed encountered problems with lines from pots or nets wrapped around their propellers, rudders or keels. If you are contemplating a circumnavigation of UK and Ireland or extended cruising in coastal waters, it is essential that you plan how to cope with a fouled propeller or rudder.

Fishing pots

Fishermen's pots are a serious hazard for yachts all round the coasts of UK and Ireland. Many are so poorly marked that you need to be very observant to spot them from a yacht cruising at 5–6 knots and even more difficult in a motor boat when you are cruising at 20 knots. Several times on the VHF we heard of boats being rescued as a result of fouled propellers. In Stonehaven we had moored next to a German couple who had to be rescued off Rattray Head because the rope from a line of pots had fouled both their propeller and steering. We came across many pots along the east coast of the UK. The best marked pots were off Stonehaven as they were marked with

Pot markers: the good, the bad and the ugly

flags and buoys and the worst were off Peterhead/Rattray Head, and those off the north-east coast of England, and Harwich. We saw every type of marker from 5-litre containers to a couple of plastic footballs in a net. It makes you think twice about sailing at night and in fog in areas where pots are around.

Pot bound off Orkney
27th June – Stromness to Pierowall

With weed starting to grow on the bottom of the hull, it was a sure sign that it was time to move on. To catch the end of the ebb, we bid farewell to Stromness at 5am, but had to motor, as there was no wind. Out through Hoy Sound, with its dramatic landscape, we had the tide with us, carrying us parallel to the coast. We made good time and I decided to go down below to take a nap but within minutes I felt the boat dramatically change course and Mags called me up on deck. I heared the panic in her voice. To my horror I saw we had a fisherman's buoy waterskiing behind us. I yelled at Mags to put the engine into neutral and to stop it. The buoy marked a lobster pot and although Mags had steered well clear of it, there was a length of floating rope which was impossible to see. It then wrapped itself around the prop and quickly rendered the engine useless. Luckily we managed to stop the engine before the rope did that. But it meant that we couldn't use the engine and there was not enough wind to sail. We were about two miles off a rocky coast with an onshore wind but we were lucky as it was very light, so we drifted in the tide. Leaning over I saw that we would not get the pot off by pulling, so I cut it loose but that still left the rope wrapped round the propeller. We had two options: call for a rescue as we couldn't sail out of danger or get into the water and cut off the rope. We had a wetsuit for exactly these kinds of emergencies. Mags donned the suit and I tied her to the boat. The water was bitterly cold and it took Mags about 10 minutes to stop hyperventilating and get control of her breathing. Thankfully the water was crystal clear so it made cutting the rope easier.

The rope had wrapped itself round the propeller and carefully missed the rope cutter. Mags needed to untangle the rope before cutting it, so decided to put the knife down; unfortunately this was not the brightest idea in 100m of water! So she came up to get another knife, this time it was the bread knife, and then returned with it tied to her wrist.

It was a great relief when both Mags and the fisherman's rope were back on the boat. We carried on our way and fortunately had no permanent damage to the engine. Westray came into sight and we passed Noup Head, our most northerly point on the trip. We passed through Papa Sound, which was very benign, despite the warning of doom from the almanac. On arrival at Pierowall we were greeted by a very friendly harbour master, Tom Rendall.

Pierowall Harbour

We had one more close encounter when we hit a pot, submerged about half a metre below the surface, right on the leading line into Helmsdale, but thankfully suffered no damage.

Pot tactics

➤ If you see a pot, always pass up tide and up wind of it, to miss any floating rope.

➤ Always make sure you brief your crew on what to do if you hit a pot or rope. If I had briefed Mags to put the engine into neutral and stop immediately, it might have prevented the rope wrapping round the propeller.

➤ Keep a full wetsuit on board and a sharp knife, so that you can cut a rope loose if the conditions allow. In stormy weather, we would not have attempted it; there is a real danger of the bottom of the boat hitting the head of the crewmember and then you have a casualty in the water, as well as a fouled propeller.

➤ When you cut off the buoy, keep hold of both ends of the rope, with some to spare if possible, so that you can cleat it off. Then at least you can try to untangle it but also, if you have tension on the line, then the swimmer can use it to pull themselves down to the propeller.

➤ Keep a long ladder onboard. We have a long swim ladder and short dinghy ladder. We nearly left the long ladder behind to save space, as we weren't planning to go swimming. We will never again consider leaving the ladder behind.

➤ Tie the knife on with a strop, or even better still, keep it in a knife sheath strapped to your leg.

Nets

Drift nets are used to catch salmon in coastal waters. They are suspended either between two large conspicuous buoys or just one buoy with a boat (often called a coble) at the inner end. They can extend up to one and a half miles in length and the nets usually have smaller floats along the line. They used to be common around Irish waters but the good news for leisure craft is that from 2006, they were banned in order to protect the dwindling numbers of wild salmon returning to rivers. The Irish Government set up a fund for the fisherman who lost their livelihood; this appears to have had the desired effect of eliminating the drift nets, according to the Irish Central Fisheries Board. They have also been banned in Scotland and so, in theory, the only place you should find them is between Whitby and Holy Island. There used to be 68 licences in England but recently the vast majority of these were bought out. However, there are still some in existence and we came across several on our trip. The cobles are recognisable either because they are speeding over to you with the fisherman waving his arms frantically, or by the tarpaulin tent covering in the bows of these small open boats. Steve Cooksey (*Gamaldansk*, Westerly GK29) got a net tangled around the rudder off Tynemouth whilst on his trip round Britain via the Caledonian Canal; he was able to clear it with a boat hook.

Previously, when cruising round Ireland, you were advised to consider how you would release yourself from a net, if it got caught on your rudder. Some people recommended carrying a pole with a Y end to push down the net. Given the ban, you may feel this is no longer necessary. Only time will tell how effective the ban will be for removing any illegal nets. However, as a good place to find salmon is around headlands and estuaries, those were the favourite place for the nets. So it may still be prudent not to plot a course from headland to headland. Also, if you are travelling at night or poor visibility, staying a minimum of five miles offshore should keep you clear. Ireland does still have a few draft nets left, in 8–10 locations in 2007, according to the Irish Central Fisheries Board. These can be found in bays or estuaries from 13 May to 31 July; these nets are smaller than drift nets in length, they have buoys at each end and usually have a team of two boats at either end.

SHIPS

You will see an increased amount of shipping around the major ports but there are some other areas to watch out for. Crossing the Humber keeps you on your toes: you are crossing three shipping lanes exiting the traffic separation scheme (TSS) roundabout. Some ports such as Humber, Harwich/Felixstowe and Portsmouth require that entry is via defined Small Vessels channels. From the Minch to the Pentland Firth, all large ships are required to radio into the coastguard when entering and leaving this stretch of water, so you get advanced warning of what is out there. We encountered several types of ships en route:

➤ *Fishing boats* The majority of the other vessels we saw were fishing boats. AIS would not be of use for many of these fishing boats as they are below the size at which AIS is legally required.
➤ *Gas rig supply ships* On the east coast, you will see many gas rig supply ships. Watch out as their superstructure (bridge) is at the bow rather than the stern, as found on many coasters and vessels elsewhere.

➤ *Ferries* We are used to those at Portsmouth. However, Dover was very busy; you need to obtain permission from the Harbour Control but with ferries entering every five to ten minutes, sailing in this area is like crossing the M25 on a zimmer frame.

➤ *Container ships* As Felixstowe is a major container port, you will see some strange sights: massive container ships with what appear to be cranes onboard. Remember that visibility from the bridge of container ships is very poor if you are close to them.

One of the saddest observations derived from our cruise was the realisation that the UK fishing industry has been completely decimated. We entered many fishing ports, where in the past, the volume of fish landed had been sizeable, yet now there were no trawlers at the quayside and their fish markets stood empty.

Submarines

You can find out which areas are being used by submarines for exercises by listening to the Subfacts broadcast issued by the coastguard on VHF and on NAVTEX. Submarine exercise areas and times of the broadcasts can be found in *Reeds Almanac* and in the Maritime Communication (NP 291 or NP289). Here is the official advice if you are sailing in an area where there are submarine exercises:

➤ Keep clear of any vessel flying the code flags NE2 (meaning that submarines are in the area).

➤ Run your engine or generator even when under sail. Submarine sonar equipment is designed to detect noise over a wide range of frequencies.

➤ Operate your echo sounder.

➤ At night, show deck level navigation lights on your pulpit and stern.

How will you know if you are being followed? You will see your depth reduce dramatically when, by checking the chart you know that it should be reading much deeper. If you alter course dramatically, the depth will return to normal. If a submarine is following you, the depth will reduce again, as it alters course to follow. According to the Fastlane Operations Room, if they are following you, it will be no less than 20m. I say this because when we were screaming along down the Sound of Sleat, in a gale force 8, we experienced exactly this. But the depth reduced to 2m. I contacted the duty Submarine Operations Room and they confirmed there were no submarines in the area. 'Maybe it was a whale' they offered ... or maybe it was Morag, Nessie's lesser known cousin!

Drilling rigs

One of the strangest sights was seeing a rig being towed in the Moray Firth. It puzzled us on watch for a long time. They are serviced in the Cromarty Firth, so in fact it is a regular sight. Most of the North Sea rigs are well offshore, except those around the Humber and off the Norfolk Coast. You will pass close to these large beasts but you must stay 500m from them.

Wind farms

The Government is committed to renewable energy, with 10 per cent of the UK electricity supplies to be generated from renewable sources of energy by 2010. Part of that will come from offshore wind farms. The blades are 22m above mean high water springs (MHWS), to ensure the safety of small recreational craft. Currently (2007) there is no safety zone around the turbines, and whilst navigation is permitted between them, it is not advised. On our cruise, we passed two of the four already built at Blyth on the sea

Scroby Sands wind farm

wall and at Scroby Sands. With 11 more already approved, or submitted for planning consent, you are bound to come across them on your trip. For more information on their location, go to www.bwea.com/offshore. The MCA has carried out trials on the effects on navigational aids and communication equipment. Their findings can be found in *Reeds Almanac*. A summary of which is:

➤ GPS, magnetic compasses, VHF, DSC and mobile phones were not affected.
➤ Loran-C: a position could not be obtained within the wind farm area.
➤ Small vessel radar performance was affected and some of the affects were that stationary vessels or other turbines could not be picked up due to blind and shadow areas. MARPA had difficulty tracking a vessel within the farm.

Wave and tidal power

The technology for harnessing the power of the sea is far less developed, with several types being trialled currently in UK waters. They are unlikely to impede your route, as they are research and development locations that can easily be avoided.

MIDGES

Midges are *definitely* a hazard on the west coast of Scotland. There is now even a midge forecast updated daily (www.midgeforecast.co.uk), with a scale of low, medium, high and nuisance. However, I don't quite understand the subtle differences between high and nuisance. The worst time is at dawn and dusk, when there is no wind. You will soon notice them biting. We barbequed once on a beach but were savaged by the midges; after that we only barbequed at anchor. Do not think of visiting the west coast without insect repellent! You will soon develop your own avoidance tactics such as only opening hatches and windows at night with the lights off.

14

ENGINE MAINTENANCE

We were surprised about the amount of time we needed to use our engine and the survey has revealed that we were not alone. On average, 54 per cent of time at sea was spent motoring or motor sailing. This has several effects: you will need a bigger budget for fuel, and you will need to factor in time and cost for engine maintenance and spares. So remember that

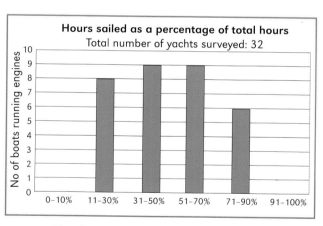

Hours sailed as a percentage of total hours
Total number of yachts surveyed: 32

whether you are in a motor boat or a sailing boat, your engine will be vitally important in achieving your cruising aims.

However, your engine is only one of many systems and pieces of equipment on board that needs to stand up to the extended use. So you need to ensure:

➤ Timely preventative maintenance
➤ Good access and visibility
➤ Correct spares are on board
➤ Access to information, skills and tools

Timely preventative maintenance

Timely preventative maintenance and regular inspection are important to keep your boat working.

➤ Do engine checks as soon as you get into harbour; don't wait until you are about to leave. This way, if you have a problem, there is a chance of getting it fixed without affecting your departure time. You will need to wait for the engine to cool to carry out some of the checks (such as oil).

➤ Devise a maintenance routine of daily, weekly and monthly checks. Ours is shown below but each boat will need its own routine tailored to the systems on board.

➤ Use protective covers whilst in harbour, eg sail cover, instrument covers etc. We failed to put on our instrument covers during a gale in harbour. Moisture got in and one instrument failed. It was all the more frustrating, as it could have been prevented.

➤ Inspect your boat regularly for any potential equipment failures.

➤ Service equipment more regularly, eg winches that you normally service annually need additional servicing en route.

➤ Service your engine regularly as prescribed in the manual.

➤ Prevent any chafing of equipment or material if possible.

	Engine –when in use	General
Daily	Check primary fuel filter for water or sediment. Check fuel levels and note engine hours. Check water level in expansion tank for fresh water system. Check engine compartment for leaks. Check oil level. Check for oil leaks. Check raw water pump for any drips. Check water strainer. Check tension on alternator belt. Turn stern grand greaser half a turn every 4–6 hours. Check stern gland.	Check sails for any signs of wear.
Weekly	Check nuts on transmission plate (due to a known problem).	Close and reopen all seacocks. Check drinking water level. Check paraffin level. Walk round the boat and check standard rigging. Grease rudder bearing (via stern greaser). Clean the heads with vinegar.
Monthly	Check gearbox oil level.	
Every 100 hours	Change impeller. Change primary fuel filter – unless you have a very rough passage – then every 50 hours. Change oil and oil filter.	

Note: as we have low-maintenance AGM batteries, there is no need for battery checks.

Good access and visibility

If essential systems are difficult to access, you are less likely to check them or, in an emergency, you will find it difficult to carry out an emergency repair. Sometimes you can improve access or visibility:

➤ Our raw water strainer has a clear top and is easy to access both in harbour and at sea. So if the engine overheats, the strainer can quickly be checked to see if it is blocked. Also we can easily see that it is clear on our daily inspection.

➤ To change the impeller on the raw water pump, we had to undo six brass screws, one of which was just below the cabin sole. This not only made it difficult to get to but also the angle at which the screw driver had to be used ensured that the brass was pared each time the pump was opened. It was difficult to remove when attached to a pontoon and impossible at sea. Replacing this with a speed seal, with easy-access knurled knobs made it simple to open at sea. (see www.speedseal.com).

➤ Our primary fuel filter not only has a glass bowl to see debris or water, but we have a white patch painted behind it on the bulkhead, so that it contrasts against anything in the glass bowl to make it easier to spot.

Correct spares on board

There is a balance between spares you carry, the space you have and the cost. It may be that in order to reduce the cost of spares, or to reduce the space required, that you reduce the spares you carry. The impact is likely to be increased time to source a spare if not available locally and possibly cost, as you are making an emergency purchase. Prior to leaving, we spoke to an engineer who has regularly worked on our engine and sought his advice on what engine spares should be carried. Allow 20 per cent contingency budget for repairs en route. The spares we carried, plus those we wished we had carried are shown here:

Spares	
Engine	**Electrical system**
Fuel filters	Bulbs for navigation lights
Oil filters	Bulbs for cabin lights
Impellers	Selection of fuses
Exhaust hose and various hoses	Insulation tape
Alternator belts	Batteries
Engine oil and empty engine oil container	Tinned electrical wire – assorted sizes
Gear box oil	Terminal ends
Outboard spark plug	Crocodile clips
Outboard oil	
Stern tube grease	

Sailing	Plumbing and cooking
Various shackles and blocks	Diaphragm pump spares
Winch grease and oil for pawls	Heads kit
Pawls and springs for winches	Baby oil to lubricate head pump
Split pins and circular clips	White vinegar for heads to prevent build up of calcium in the pipes
Line to make up either halyard/ topping lift	Spares for cooker eg spare gas regulator or paraffin cooker spares
Sail spares: batterns, battern ends, sliders	
Sails: carried old genoa. Stored old main with a relative which could be sent if needed	

General	
Spares for autohelm (belts, bracket)	Whipping twine – multiple colours
WD40	Varying sizes of elastic cord
Team McLube	Assorted stainless screws (marine grade)
Lithium grease spray	Assorted jubilee clips
Vaseline	Seizing wire
3 in 1 oil	Assorted nuts and bolts (marine grade)
Epoxy kit	Duct tape
Underwater setting sealant	Self-amalgamating tape
Sealant	Anti-rust paint
Wood glue	Miscellaneous eg door catch
Marine catalogues	

Spares we wish we had carried	Comments
A complete water pump	The bearings on the water pump failed which required specialist tools and the correct-sized bearings. Carrying a whole pump means you can replace it yourself and you don't have to wait for the bearings to arrive
Exhaust elbow	These fail about every five years
Car exhaust bandage	Temporary repair for a leaking exhaust elbow

Carry a couple of catalogues from mail order companies, so that if you need a spare it can be sent at a reasonable price. Some are available on CD; this will help you to save space.

Access to information, skills and tools

The harbour masters are a mine of useful information about local experts. They will know where to find the right expertise – often in surprising places. We had neither the tools nor the knowledge to remove a sheared and seized alternator bolt, but we found both at a local scallop gear manufacturer. Make sure you take all the equipment manuals with you. We were able to diagnose a problem and confirm that it could be left without any issue, by contacting the manufacturer over the phone. The manual will give you the contact numbers. These are all the tools that we took with us:

Tools and repair equipment	
Easy to access tools	**Riggers tool kit**
Screwdrivers: flat head and Philips	Bosun's chair
Adjustable spanner: small	Knife
LED head torch and hand torch	Zippo lighter
Pliers	Lighter fluid
Scissors	Sail maker's palm
Tape measure	Several needles stored in oiled paper
Knife	Waxed thread
Power tools	**Electricians tool kit**
12v or mains drill	Multimeter
Drill bits: metal and wood	Wire cutters
	Crimper
	Electrical testing screwdriver
General tool kit	
Bradawl	Chisel
Metric and imperial socket set	Spanner for stern tube
Paint brush	Oil filter extractor
Epoxy kit	File
Hand saw	Sandpaper and sanding block
Multi-sized allen keys	Hammer
Multi-sized screwdrivers (flat and Philips)	Long-nosed pliers
Large adjustable spanner	Metal ruler
Flexible nut spanner	Any tools required for your cooker
Long grabber tool	Baby's nappies – excellent for cleaning up engine oil, cleaning the bilges etc

The last day
22nd August – Dover to Gosport

We left Dover with the most spectacular sunrise over the white cliffs –it made getting up at 4:30 seem worth it. With a NW F4/F5, Ituna picked up her skirts and we were screaming along at 8.5 knots. We passed Dungeness power station (I wondered about writing a book: nuclear power stations we have passed ... Windscale, Sizewell etc ...) The wind soon died but at least it stayed NW – until about half way to the magnificent chalky cliffs of Beachy Head. We still had the tide with us, so at least we were making progress, despite the wind being dead on the nose. But then the tide turned ... and we sailed depressingly slowly; it was at this point we started singing. We decided to press on and not go into Brighton, as the wind would be even stronger from the same direction the next day – so we would go even slower!

Portsmouth's Spinnaker Tower was visible for a long way out, like a beacon. At times it was depressing because it was so far away, yet welcoming as it was our finish line. It stands just inside the entrance of the narrow harbour, and at 2am when we passed, it was swathed in purple light. We had very mixed emotions: elated that we had finished, yet tinged with sadness that our adventure was over. For me, there was also a touch of relief that we had arrived back safely – as skipper you are always responsible for whatever happens on board, and it was brought home by the Mayday that we heard during the day. The body of a yachtsman had been found at sea, just south of where we were with no sign of the yacht.

But for us this had been an amazing experience, something that we would treasure for the rest of our lives.

Sunrise over the White Cliffs of Dover and Portsmouth Spinnaker Tower – our finish line

APPENDIX 1
CHARTS

Charts taken for our route:

Gosport – Yarmouth – Dartmouth – Salcombe – Falmouth – Helford – Penzance – Padstow – Dale – Neyland – Dale – Fishguard – Holyhead – Kirkcudbright – Campbeltown – Torrisdale Bay – Tarbert – Ardrishaig – Bellanoch Bridge – Crinan – Tobernochy – Puilladobhrain – Kerrera – Tobermory – Arisaig – Kyleakin – Loch Gairloch – Loch Inver – Kinlochbervie – Stromness – Pierowall – Calf Sound (Eday) – Stronsay - Sanday –– Shapinsay – Kirkwall – Wick – Helmsdale – Inverness – Lossiemouth – Whitehills – Peterhead – Stonehaven – Arbroath – Eyemouth – Holy Island – Amble – Blyth – Newcastle – Whitby – Lowestoft – Pin Mill – Walton Backwaters – Dover – Gosport

Ref	Title: Imray Charts	Used	Comments
C51	Cardigan Bay	Y	♣ 5620
C62	Irish Sea	Y	
C23	Fifeness to Inverness	Y	
C24	Flamborough Head to Fifeness	N	Not needed
C13	River Cleddau-Milford Haven to Haverfordwest	Y	
C27	Firth of Forth	N	Not visited
C63	Firth of Clyde	Y	
C29	Harwich to Whitby	Y	
C68	North Scotland and Orkneys	Y	

Ref	Title: Admiralty Folios	Used	Comments
5600	The Solent and Approaches	Y	
5601	East Devon and Dorset coast, Exmouth to Christchurch	Y	
5602	The West Country, Falmouth to Teignmouth	Y	
5610	The Firth of Clyde	Y	
5603	Falmouth to Padstow including Isles of Scilly	Y	
5605	Western approaches to the Dover Strait	Y	
5607	Thames Estuary and Suffolk coast	Y	
5611	West coast of Scotland Mull of Kintyre Ardnamurchan	Y	
5609	North West Wales including Menai Strait	Y	

Ref	Title: Admiralty Charts	Used	Comments
1178	Approaches to the Bristol Channel	Y	♣ 5608
1164	Hartland Point to Ilfracombe including Lundy	N	♣ 5608
1160	Harbours in Somerset and North Devon	N	♣ 5608
1478	Saint Govan's Head to St David's Head	Y	♣ 5620
1482	Plans on the south and west coasts of Dyed	N	♣ 5620
1973	Cardigan Bay: southern part	Y	♣ 5620
1410	St George Channel	N	Not needed
2696	Plans in the Isle of Man	N	♣ 5613
2198	North Channel: southern part/Portpatrick	Y	♣ 5612
2199	North Channel: northern part	N	♣ 5612
2878	Approaches to Milford Haven	Y	♣ 5620
2094	Kirkcudbright to Mull of Galloway and Isle of Man	Y	♣ 5613
1344	Kirkcudbright Bay	Y	♣ 5613
1396	Solway Firth and approaches	N	Not needed
1753	Belfast Lough and approaches	N	♣ 5612
1791	Caledonian Canal	N	Not visited
2541	Lochs on the West of Scotland	N	Not visited
2540	Loch Aish and approaches	Y	
2498	Inner Sound: southern part	Y	
2534	Plans on west coast of Scotland	N	Not visited
2207	Point of Ardnamurchan to the Sound of Sleat	Y	
2208	Mallaig to Canna Harbour	Y	
2209	Inner Sound	Y	
2210	Approaches to Inner Sound	Y	
2479	Inner Sound: northern part	N	Not needed
1794	North Minch: southern part	Y	
2528	Loch Gairloch and Loch Kishorn to Strome Narrows	Y	
2501	Summer Isles	N	Not visited
2502	Eddrachillis Bay	N	Not needed
2500	Approaches to Ullapool	N	Not visited
2509	Rubha Reidh to Cailleach Head	N	Not needed
2504	Approaches to Lochinver	Y	
3146	Loch Ewe	N	Not visited
2503	Approaches to Kinlochbervie	Y	

1785	North Minch: northern part	Y	
2076	Loch Eriboll	N	Not visited
2568	Harbours in Orkney Isles	Y	
2250	Orkney Isles: eastern sheet	Y	
2584	Approaches to Kirkwall	Y	
1553	Bay of Kirkwall	N	Not needed
2562	Plans in the northern Orkney Islands	Y	
2249	Orkney Isles: western sheet	Y	
2581	Southern approaches to Scapa Flow	N	
2162	Pentland Firth and approaches	N	Not visited
1407	Montrose to Berwick-upon-Tweed	Y	Not visited
1462	Harbours on the north and east coasts of Scotland	Y	
222	Buckie to Fraserburgh	Y	
1409	Buckie to Arbroath	Y	
111	Berwick on Tweed to the Farne Islands	Y	
L160	St Abb's Head to the Farne Islands	Y	
1612	Harbours and anchorages to east coast of England and Scotland	Y	
1191	River Tyne to Flamborough Head	Y	
L121	Flamborough Head to Withernsea	Y	♣ 5614
134	Rivertees to Scarborough	Y	
109	River Humber and the Rivers Ouse and Trent	Y	♣ 5614
L107	East Coast: approaches to the River Humber	Y	♣ 5614
L108	Approaches to The Wash	N	♣ 5614
1503	Outer Dowsing to Smiths Knoll including Indefatigable Banks	N	♣ 5614
1536	Approaches to Great Yarmouth and Lowestoft	Y	♣ 5614
1543	Wintertonness to Orford Ness	N	♣ 5614

♣ = now replaced by leisure folio
L = leisure series

APPENDIX 2
PILOT BOOKS AND SAILING DIRECTIONS

Ref	Admiralty pilots	Area
NP 27	*Channel Pilot*	Scilly Isles, Cape Cornwall to Bognor Regis
NP 28	*Dover Strait Pilot*	Bognor Regis to Southwold
NP 54	*North Sea (West) Pilot*	Southwold to Rattray Head
NP 52	*North Coast of Scotland Pilot*	North and north-east coast of Scotland, Orkneys, Shetland, Faeroe Island and Caledonian Canal
NP 66	*West Coast of Scotland Pilot*	Mull of Galloway to Cape Wrath
NP 37	*West Coast of England and Wales Pilot*	South-west Scottish Cape Cornwall to Mull of Galloway including the Isle of Man
NP 40	*Irish Coast Pilot*	Coastal waters around Ireland

Sea Area	Other pilot books and other useful publications	Comments
UK, Channel Islands and Ireland	*Reeds Nautical Almanac*	Provides all the data required to navigate Atlantic coastal waters around the UK, Ireland, Channel Islands and selected parts of Europe
Ireland	*South and West Coasts Ireland Irish Cruising Club (ICC) Sailing Directions*	Carnsore Point (SE) to Bloody Foreland (NW)
	East and North Coasts of Ireland ICC Sailing Directions	Carnsore Point (SE) up to Bloody Foreland (NE)
Irish Sea	*Lundy Irish Sea Pilot* David Taylor (Imray)	Lands End to Portpatrick including Lundy and Isle of Man. This doesn't cover the Irish or Northern Irish coast.
	Cruising Anglesey and Adjoining Waters Ralph Morris	Anglesey, and the Menai Strait, Liverpool to Pwllheli
West coast of Scotland	*Solway Sailing Directions*	Solway Coast from Ravenglass around to Portpatrick, including rounding the Mull of Galloway. Available from: W Matheson, Honorary Secretary South West Sailing Association, Anchorlea, 70 Main Street, Isle of Whithorn, Newton Stewart DG8 8LG Tel: 01988 500375 Cost £7.50
	Firth of Clyde Sailing Directions Clyde Cruising Club (CCC)	Whitehaven to Mull of Kintyre to Upper Loch Fyne, Bangor to Rathlin Island, Isle of Man
	Isle of Mull and adjacent coast Martin Lawrence	North Sound of Jura to Ardnamurchan Point and from Tiree across to Fort William, includes only Corpach sea lock of Caledonian Canal.

	Kintyre to Ardnamurchan CCC Sailing Directions	Mull of Kintyre to Ardnamurchan including the islands of Islay, Jura, Colonsay, Mull, Tiree, Coll and Gigha.
	Clyde to Colonsay Martin Lawrence (Imray)	Mull of Galloway to Islay to Colonsay to Crinan to Upper Loch Fyne. Includes Crinan Canal, most of Jura bar (very northern corner) but excludes Northern Irish ports.
North-west Coast of Scotland	*Ardnamurchan Point to Cape Wrath* CCC Sailing Directions	Ardnamurchan Point to Cape Wrath, including Inner Hebrides north of Ardnamurchan excludes Outer Hebrides
	Skye and Northwest Scotland Martin Lawrence (Imray)	
Western Isles	*Outer Hebrides* Sailing Directions CCC	Outer Hebrides from Butt of Lewis to Barra Head includes St Kilda Group
	The Western Isles Martin Lawrence (Imray)	
Northern Isles	*Shetland Islands* Sailing Directions CCC	Covers Shetland Islands and Fair Isle
North and north-east Scotland	*North and East Scotland* Martin Lawrence (Imray)	Blyth to Cape Wrath including the Caledonian Canal, Forth and Forth Canal, Union Canal, Farne Islands, Firth of Forth and Pentland Firth but excludes Orkneys
	N and NE Coasts of Scotland and Orkney Islands CCC Sailing Directions	Cape Wrath to Peterhead, includes Orkneys Islands, rounding Cape Wrath and Caledonian Canal.
East Coast	Royal Northumberland Yacht Club (RNYC) Sailing Directions Humber to Rattray Head	Humber to Rattray Head Available from RNYC E-mail steward@rnyc.org.uk
	Forth, Tyne, Dogger, Humber Henry Irving (Imray)	Blakeney to St Abbs
	East Coast Pilot Colin Jarman, Garth Cooper, Dick Holness (Imray)	Lowestoft to Ramsgate
	East Coast Rivers Jack Coote	Southwold to the Swale
	Suffolk Rivers Deben and Ore	The latest sketch maps showing the entrances to River Ore and Deben can be downloaded from www.Eastcoastrivers.com. This site will also soon cover Southwold. It is available for a small charge from Small Craft Deliveries Ltd, 12 Quay Street, Woodbridge, Suffolk, IP12 1BX Tel 01394 382600

South Coast	*The Shell Channel Pilot* **Tom Cunliffe**	From Ramsgate to the Isles of Scilly, and from Dunkerque to L'Aber-Wrac'h
	Yachting Monthly West Country Cruising Companion **Mark Fishwick**	Portland Bill to Padstow Including Isles of Scilly
Isles of Scilly	*Royal Cruising Club Pilotage Foundation The Isles of Scilly Pilot* **Robin Brandon, John and Fay Garey (Imray)**	The Isles of Scilly

APPENDIX 3
MARINAS IN NORTH-WEST IRELAND AND SCOTLAND

North-west Ireland

Cruising north-west Ireland and Scotland will need careful planning if you intend to leave your boat in a marina for the winter.

South, east and north-east coasts of both Ireland and Scotland are well served for marinas and hence omitted from the map.

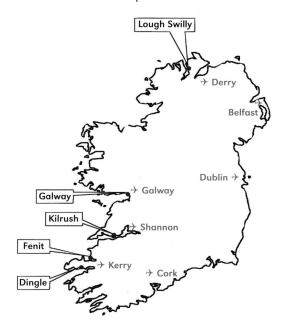

Marina location	Facilities	Transport
Lough Swilly Marina 00353 (0)74 9360008 www.loughswillymarina.ie	Afloat only	Approx 10min drive from Derry airport to marina. Daily flights from East Midlands, Glasgow, Liverpool and London Stansted to Derry airport.
Galway Marina 00353 (0)86 3379304	Storage ashore	Short taxi ride from Galway airport to marina. Daily flights to Dublin, Luton, Manchester, Edinburgh to Galway airport.
Kilrush Marina 00353 (0)65 9052072 www.kilrushcreekmarina.ie	Storage ashore (some under cover)	Approx 1 hr drive from Shannon Airport to marina. Daily flights from low cost operators to Shannon from London (Heathrow. Stansted, Luton, Gatwick), Liverpool, Nottingham, Manchester and Glasgow (Prestwick).
Fenit Harbour Marina 00353 (0)66 7136231 www.fenitharbour.com/ marina.html	Afloat only	Approx 45min drive from Kerry airport and Dingle is one hour away. Flights from low cost operators to Kerry airport from Dublin, London, Liverpool or Manchester.
Dingle Marina 00353 (0)66 9151629 www.dinglemarina.com	Afloat only	

North-west Scotland

The coast below Oban is well served with Adfern marina and the many marinas in the Firth of Clyde. In between Oban and the Orkneys there are buoys and some pontoons, eg single pontoons at Loch Gairloch, Loch Inver and Kyleakin but these are often crowded. North-east coast well served with Wick, Inverness and Peterhead.

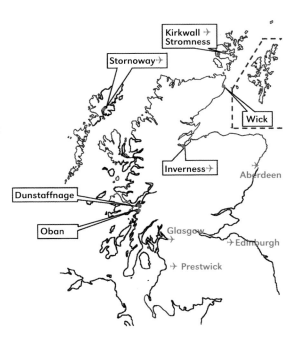

Marina location	Facilities	Transport
Oban Marina Located on Kerrera (an island opposite Oban). 01631 565 333 www.obanmarina.com	Storage ashore (some under cover)	Approx 3hrs by train or bus from Glasgow airport. Low cost operators fly to Glasgow and Prestwick. Some buses go from Glasgow airport to Oban. Distance: 100 miles to Glasgow, 200 miles to Carlisle. Oban Marina run regular ferry service to and from Oban. There is a seaplane that operates straight to Oban from Glasgow. Berth holders get 25% discount www.lochlomandseaplanes.com
Dunstaffnage Marina (3 miles from Oban) 01631 566555 www.dunstaffnagemarina. co.uk	Storage ashore	
Stornoway Marina 01851702688	Some storage ashore	Flights from Aberdeen, Inverness, Edinburgh and Glasgow.
Orkney Marinas: Kirkwall, Stromness 01856 871313 www.orkneymarinas.co.uk	Afloat facilities only	Logan Air operates to Kirkwall from Glasgow, Edinburgh, Inverness and Aberdeen. Ferries from Wick, Scrabster and Aberdeen arrive at Stromness
Inverness Inverness Marina 01752 6446348 www.invernessmarina.com In the canal: Seaport Marina 01463 725500 Caley Marine 01463 233437	All facilities except Caley Marine are afloat	Regular flights from most main UK cities to Inverness.
Wick 01955 602030 www.wickharbour.co.uk	Some storage ashore	Regular flights to Wick airport from many UK cities.

APPENDIX 4
KAYAK CIRCUMNAVIGATIONS

Circumnavigators by kayak, plus any websites or books about their trips:

➤ Bill Taylor, with Mick Wibrew and Richard Elliott completed the first circumnavigation of both Britain and Ireland in 1986. *Commitment and Open Crossings: First Circumnavigation of Britain and Ireland by Kayak* Bill Taylor.
➤ *Simon Williams* completed the journey in 2002 in memory of his brother who had died of leukaemia at the age of 13 and raised £20,000 for Leukaemia Research Fund.
➤ *Sean Morley* paddled round the UK and Ireland in 2004. www.expeditionkayak.com/
➤ *Stuart Fisher* detailed his 15 year journey in his book *Inshore Britain.*
➤ *Harry Whelan, Barry Shaw and Phil Clegg* are considered to have been the fastest team around Britain in 2005, completing the circumnavigation in 80 days. Paul Caffyn and Nigel Dennis were first sea kayakers to circumnavigate Britain in 1980 in 85 days. http://en.wikipedia.org/wiki/Sea_kayak

APPENDIX 5
FUEL COSTS AND AVAILABILITY

The diesel costs for our trip in 2006 are give below. Whilst cost of fuel will change, it gives you an indication of the relative costs and the advantage of refuelling at commercial refuelling points.

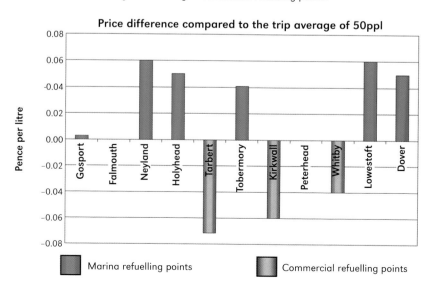

	Waterside refuelling	Fuel available in cans
S Coast England	Fairly regularly available, with careful planning refuelling only at waterside possible	
W Coast England	Conway, Pwllheli, Cardiff, Portishead	
W Coast Scotland	Tobermory (Cal Mac pier), Largs, Holy Loch Marina, Kirkcudbright	
Ireland	Malahide, Dun Laoghaire	Howth
Northern Ireland	Bangor	
N & E Coast Scotland		Lossiemouth
E & NE Coast England	Ramsgate, Gillingham, Burnham, Bradwell (R Blackwater), Levington (R Orwell), Hull, Newcastle (Royal Quays)	Brightlingsea

Table showing quayside availability of petrol in 2007. If you require petrol please check that these ports still have petrol as the availability will gradually reduce.

APPENDIX 6
BOOKS, ARTICLES AND WEBSITES

Books
Circumnavigations
England and lowland Scotland via Firth and Forth Canal
E E Middleton *The Cruise of the Kate*
Round Britain via Cape Wrath
Libby Purves *One Summer's Grace*
John McCarthy and Sandi Toksvig *Island Race*
Stan Lester *Around the Island: Britain in a Hundred Days*
Round Britain via Caledonian Canal
Ellen MacArthur *Taking on the World*
Jonathan Raban *Coasting*
UK and Ireland
Ray and Margo Glaister *UK Circumnavigation*
Tim Batstone *Round Britain Windsurf*

General
Brian Fagan *Staying Put! The Art of Anchoring*
Report by QinetiQ 'Performance Investigation of Marine Radar Reflectors on the Market' commissioned by the MAIB
Nigel Calder *Boatowner's Mechanical and Electrical Manual*, Adlard Coles Nautical

Harold Barre *Managing 12 Volts*
Jill Schinas *Kids in the Cockpit: A Pilot Book to Safe and Happy Sailing with Children*,
Adlard Coles Nautical
RYA Flags and Visual Signals

Tourist and wildlife guides
Hamish Haswell–Smith, *The Scottish Islands. An indispensable guide to the Scottish Islands* covering wildlife, scenery, maps, history and facts about all the Islands.
Charlie Connelly, *Attention all Shipping – A journey round the shipping forecast.* A humorous yet informative cruise around the shipping forecast areas, covering the history of many of the sea areas you will pass through.
Hadoram Shirihai and Brett Jarrett, *Whales, Dolphins and Seals – A Field Guide to the Marine Mammals of the World*
Hilary Burn, Peter Holden, J T R Sharrock, *The RSPB Guide to British Birds*
The Rough Guides: Great Britain, England, Scotland, Ireland, Wales
Christopher Somerville, *Coast – A Celebration of Britain's Coastal Heritage*
Christopher Somerville, *Coast – The Journey Continues*

Weather
Alan Watts *Instant Weather Forecasting*, Adlard Coles Nautical
Chris Tibbs *RYA Weather*
Mike Harris *Understanding Weatherfax*, Adlard Coles Nautical
Simon Keeling *The Sailor's Book of the Weather*

Safety
RYA *Sea Survival*
RNLI: *Sea Safety The Complete Guide*
Frances and Michael Howorth *The Grab Bag Book*, Adlard Coles Nautical
K Adlard Coles *Heavy Weather Sailing* edited by Peter Bruce, Adlard Coles Nautical
Colin Berry, Douglas Justins *First Aid at Sea*, Adlard Coles Nautical

Magazine articles
Yachts
England and lowland Scotland via Firth and Forth Canal
Jim Mottram *Singlehanded to Scotland – Sailing Today*, June 2007
Round Britain via Cape Wrath
Roger Oliver *Single-handed Round Britain – PBO*, December 2003, January 20 04. To be published by Adlard Coles Nautical as a book with other articles: *Sailing Around the UK*
Ken Endean *Yachting Monthly*, March–November 2005
UK and Ireland
Roger Oliver *Second Time Around – PBO*, January 2005–February 2006
Round Britain via Caledonian Canal
John and Sue Chadwick *Part time around Britain – Yachting Monthly*, April and May 2006
Sam Brunner *What Katie Did – Yachting Monthly*, November 2006
Katie Miller *Once Around the Block – Sailing Today*, December 2006, January 2007

Motorboats
Round Britain via Cape Wrath
Dominic and Nicola Gribbin *Living the Dream – Motor Boats Monthly*, December 2004
Rob Andrews *Fairey Ring – Motor Boats Monthly*, June 2002
Wendy and Maurice Walmsley, Malcolm and Glenda Stennett *Over the Top – Motor Boat and Yachting*, February, March and April 1996
Stanley Ross *Roundabout Way, Motor Boat and Yachting*, June 2002
Round Britain via the Caledonian Canal
Brian Rhodes *65 a Day – Motor Boat and Yachting*, May 1991
Mike Perry *Roundabout Route – Motor Boats Monthly* January 1997

RIBs
Round Britain via Cape Wrath
John Walker and Paul Mahy *Rough Riders – Motor Boats Monthly*, September 1999
Yvonne Mackintosh *Bouncing round Britain – Motor Boats Monthly*, April 2001

Websites
Yachts
www.ituna.info/
http://home.clara.net/rayglaister/
www.2oldgitsinaboat.co.uk
www.soundsailing.co.uk/
www.rnli.org.uk
www.summersailing.co.uk/

www.zoneseekers.com/karen/
www.ab2004.co.uk
http://sailroundbritain.blogspot.com
http://homepages.rya-online.net/oliver/
www.sailtales.co.uk/st-fun-vvab-2005.php
www.co26-around-uk.co.uk

Motor Boats/RIBs
www.seeroundbritain.com/

http://passageofhope.blogspot.com

Weather
www.franksingleton.clara.net

Canal licence information
www.waterscape.com

INDEX